CHARACTER BUILDERS

Respect for Self and Others

A K-6 CHARACTER EDUCATION PROGRAM

- Monthly Themes
- Literature and Vocabulary Selections
- Skill Building
- Ready-to-Implement Activities
- School or Classroom Character Theme Posters
- Puppets, Activities, and Stories Adapted for Younger Children with "Admiral," the Moon Puppet
- Integrated Literacy
- Cooperative Learning Structures

Dr. Michele Borba

ʃ

Jalmar Press

Character Builders: Respect for Self and Others

Copyright © 2001 by Michele Borba, Ed.D.

Jalmar Press
Permission's Department
P. O. Box 1185
Torrance, CA 90505
(310) 816-3085 Fax: (310) 816-3092 e-mail: jalmar@worldnet.att.net
Website: www.jalmarpress.com

Published by Jalmar Press

Character Builders: Respect for Self and Others
A K-6 Character Education Program

Author: Dr. Michele Borba
Editor and Story Writer: Marie Conte
Project Director: Jeanne Iler
Cover Design and Composition: Jeanne Iler
Interior Illustrations: Bob Burchett

Manufactured in the United States of America

10 9 8 7 6 5 4 3 2 1
ISBN: 1-880396-55-6

Contents

Contents

5   Listening With Respect   91

Contents

Introduction

Building Character in Students

It's great to be great, but it's greater to be human.
—LUCY M. MONTGOMERY

In my consulting tours of school sites one experience became all too common. I'd walk into a classroom and notice a rule chart clearly posted with pre-established student expectations. Then I'd quietly walk up to a student, and choose one of the rules to quiz him on the meaning. The conversation generally went like this: "One of the rules on the chart says you are to act respectfully at this school. What does respect mean?" All too frequently the student's response would be a "shrug of the shoulders" or a simple "I don't know." I'd prod the student a bit further: "But it says you're supposed to act respectfully. Can you tell me what that looks like and sounds like?" "I don't know," the student would say.

What I just described is an all too common trend. Far too many of today's students do not know the meaning, behavior, and value of some of the most critical traits of solid character. And, there's a significant reason why: character traits, like skills, are learned. One of the primary ways students acquire these traits is by watching others do them right. Reflect on that statement a minute and ask yourself: "Who are my students watching to learn these traits?" Over the past few years we've witnessed a breakdown of appropriate role models for today's youth. Some of the primary sources that used to nurture the character of our students have broken down: the home, the neighborhood block, community support agencies, even the schools have become larger and less personalized. Role models for today's students are frankly atrocious. I watch in horror as a professional baseball player on national television is allowed to spit in an umpire's face and not be held accountable. I'm astounded when rock stars and authors of some of the most hateful lyrics I've ever heard receive standing ovations. I'm amazed that so many actors (some without even a high school diploma) are given contracts that quadruple the salary of the President of the United States. The breakdown of appropriate role models for our youth is clearly an enormous educational handicap.

The breakdown of appropriate role models is certainly not the only reason for the decline in solid character development of our youth. Dr. Thomas Lickona cites ten troubling trends among youth in our society that point to an overall moral decline. Over the past decades these ten indicators, which have been increasing significantly, show a failure of our students in the acquisition and development of character:

Youth Trends and Moral Decline

1. Violence and vandalism.

2. Stealing.

3. Cheating.

4. Disrespect for authority.

5. Peer cruelty.

6. Bigotry.

7. Bad language.

8. Sexual precocity and abuse.

9. Increasing self-centeredness and declining civic responsibility.

10. Self-destructiveness.

Dr. Thomas Lickona: Educating for Character. Bantam: 1991. p. 16-18.

"Sow an act, and you reap a habit. Sow a habit, and you reap a character. Sow a character, and you reap a destiny."

—Charles Reade

What can help turn these trends around? A recent poll revealed that 86% of adults surveyed believed that the number one purpose of public schools, apart from providing a basic education, is "to prepare students to be responsible citizens" (*Learning,* March/April 1997, page 3).

The truth is that school may well be the last beacon of hope for many of our students. How else will they have a chance to understand the value of traits called "responsibility" or "caring" or "respect" or "peacemaking" or "cooperation?" How else will these youths have the opportunity to watch someone model the trait appropriately? How else but at school will many of our students be able to learn these core skills they will need to succeed in every arena of their lives? Your power in your role of "educator" is extraordinary. The simple but profound truth is: How else but from a caring, committed teacher will many of today's students have a chance to expand their personal, social, and academic potential? This series, called *Character Builders,* will show you how.

Character Builders is purposely designed to be used in many ways. Each Character Builder can be infused into almost any subject. The themes have been carefully chosen based not only on research in character development but also in self-esteem theory. Each Character

Builder teaches students not only the trait but also a few core skills that will optimize their chances of success not only in school but also in life. The dream of educators is to have students who are more responsible, respectful, cooperative, peaceable and caring. Where do you begin? The key to enhancing student character development I believe is found in three critical premises. Above all else, keep these three premises in mind:

Premises of Character Development

- Character traits are learned.

- Character traits are changeable.

- Educators are able to create the conditions that enhance such change because they can control the learning environment and their attitude.

Let's analyze each one of these premises. Each one is important to understand if we want to enhance the character development of our students:

Character traits are learned. To the best of my scientific knowledge there are no genes for character development and self-esteem; none of our students are born with strong character. Instead, our children have acquired their character and self-esteem through repeated experiences in their pasts. Too often, the critical skills that enhance the core Character Builders have not been modeled or emphasized for students. You can make a difference for your students by deliberately modeling the traits and by providing them with opportunities to learn these skills.

> "Show me the man you honor, and I will know what kind of man you are."
>
> —Thomas Carlyle

Character traits are changeable. From the premise that character development is learned, a second principle arises naturally and unavoidably: If character traits are learned, therefore we can teach them and change them. It is essential to keep this concept in mind because it means that educators and parents do have tremendous power to teach critical skills and traits that optimize students' chances of success not only now but for the rest of their lives.

Educators are able to create the conditions that enhance such change because they can control the environment and their attitude. If character traits and skills are learned and changeable, then educators have the ability to create those changes by means of their attitudes, their curriculum content and the atmosphere they create. What is needed is the knowledge of what skills are most important to enhance each trait and which traits we should deliberately accentuate and model to help students "catch" the attitudes. That's what *Character Builders* is all about . . . and we haven't a moment to lose!

Character Builders is based on the same premises as *Esteem Builders: A K-8 Curriculum for Improving Student Achievement, Behavior and School Climate* that I published in 1989. The esteem-building series includes manuals for school, home, staff and workshop training, all designed to provide a comprehensive approach to developing high self-esteem in students. *Character Builders* is the next step in teaching students the skills that will help them succeed. The five core Character Builders complement the Esteem Builders for high self-esteem, namely: Security, Selfhood, Affiliation, Mission, and Competence. These five components serve as the foundation for enhancing students' positive self-perceptions, thereby encouraging the development of their potential and confidence in learning. The esteem building blocks have been sequenced within each character building theme to ensure that students will acquire these skills as well. It is strongly recommended that the themes within this manual be presented in the order in which they were written. This is the best way to ensure students' acquisition of the skills and character building traits. The five core Character Builders in this series are listed below along with their corresponding Esteem Builders.

Five Core Esteem and Character Builders

Esteem Builder Trait

Security
A feeling of comfort and safety; being able to trust others.

Selfhood
A feeling of individuality; acquiring an accurate and realistic self-description.

Affiliation
A feeling of belonging, acceptance or relatedness.

Mission
A feeling of purpose and motivation in life; setting achievable goals.

Social Competence
A feeling of success when relationships are handled respectfully and responsibly.

Character Builder Trait

Responsibility and Trustworthiness
Doing what is right; being answerable and accountable to yourself and others.

Respect
Treating yourself and others in a courteous and considerate manner.

Cooperation
Respectfully working with others in a fair and equitable manner to accomplish mutual goals.

Peaceability
Solving conflicts in a peaceful and responsible manner; building solid citizenship skills.

Caring
Showing concern and sensitivity for the needs and feelings of others; being compassionate and empathetic.

The activities in this book have been organized around six core universal moral values outlined by a group of twenty-nine youth leaders and educators at what has come to be known as the "Aspen Conference." The six core values are:

- Trustworthiness

- Respect

- Responsibility

- Justice and Fairness

- Caring

- Civic Virtue and Citizenship

"We don't
know
who we
are until
we see
what we
can do."
—Martha
Grimes

IMPLEMENTING THE PROGRAM

Character Builders is designed to be used in many ways, including:

- on a daily or month-by-month or bi-monthly basis;

- on a weekly or bi-weekly basis, where lessons are taught either by the homeroom teacher or an outside trained staff member; and,

- on a periodic basis, where the activities can serve as enrichment.

For maximum results with this program, it is strongly recommended that each Character Builder be focused upon for a minimum of six weeks to two months. Each trait introduces at least five critical skills that not only enhance the trait's acquisition but also students' social and personal competence. *Character Builders* is also most effective when implemented school-wide. The flow sequence for implementing the six core traits for an entire school year would look like this:

Character Builder Monthly Planner										
	Sep	Oct	Nov	Dec	Jan	Feb	Mar	Apr	May	Jun
• Responsibility & Trustworthiness	▬▬▬▬▬▬									
• Respect		▬▬▬▬▬▬								
• Cooperation & Fairness				▬▬▬▬▬▬						
• Peaceability & Citizenship						▬▬▬▬▬▬				
• Caring								▬▬▬▬▬		

SCHOOL-WIDE CHARACTER BUILDING

Many schools have found that emphasizing a different Character Builder theme school-wide for a month or six weeks (or more) is a highly successful way for students to acquire these new skills. Focusing at least a month on the same theme allows everyone in the school (staff as well as students) to be aware of the same key concepts. Keep in mind many schools have chosen to implement a Character Builder theme each quarter, some on a semester basis, and a few select one each academic year. The time frame should be determined by the desires of the staff. The value of "shared targeting" is powerful. When everyone at the site is reinforcing and modeling the same behavior, students are much more likely to learn a new Character Builder trait and use the skill in their life.

SPECIAL FEATURES OF CHARACTER BUILDERS

The activities in the *Character Builders* series have been developed for students from grade K through 6. As this encompasses a wide range of ages, wherever possible specific ways to adapt the activity for older or younger students are noted. Puppet stories for younger children are in gray tone and accompanied by an image of a puppet. Any activity can be scaled down for younger nonreading/nonwriting students by using pictorial answers or dictating their responses for them. The activity can also easily be converted to a "class meeting" in which responses are reported verbally.

The five manuals in the *Character Builders* series are designed for sequential use. Each manual addresses a distinct character trait and the skills needed to enhance that trait. The manuals are designed to be used as an entire program for a school year (though some schools choose one trait for an entire school year!) Whenever possible, teachers should provide relevant examples of the trait as they materialize in context or in course content.

Common to each manual are the following activities:

Character Builder Posters. Each of the five *Character Builders* in this series—Responsibility, Respect, Cooperation, Peaceability and Caring—is illustrated by a poster that can be hung in the classroom (and ideally school walls). The form in the book can be enlarged to a size of at least a 18" × 22". If implementing a school-wide character development program, consider making multiple copies of the posters and then hanging them in dozens of locations, such as the cafeteria, faculty room, halls, restrooms, library, and school office. Place the Character Builder Posters on each teacher's door as well as the doors of the school nurse, secretary, custodians, media specialists and even the school bus driver. The more the Character Builder is accentuated, the greater the likelihood people will "catch the theme." Provide students with a copy of the poster to store in their Character Builder Notebook.

Call Jalmar Press at (800) 662-9662 for a descriptive brochure about *Character Builders* manuals.

Character Builder Notebooks. It is strongly recommended that each student keep a spiral 1/2" notebook to store all completed Character Builder activities. A set of five indexed dividers for each student could separate each of the five core Character Builder traits. A cover for the notebook is found on page RT1c for duplication.

Looks Like/Sounds Like Charts. Each character trait in this series is accompanied by four to five essential skills to teach students. One of the techniques in *Character Builders* used to teach students a new skill is the "looks like/sounds like" chart. Students may then make a copy of the chart on an individual "looks like/sounds like" form provided in the manual and then store it in their Character Builder Notebooks. A set of eyes for "Looks Like" and ears for "Sounds Like" are provided on pages RT1f and RT1g to adapt the chart for younger students.

Go/Stop Language. To help students recognize appropriate and inappropriate language and behaviors for each character building theme, an activity called Go/Stop Language—or "stoppers" and "starters"—is included. Go and Stop Signs may easily be converted into stick puppets for role playing with younger children.

Class Meetings. One of the most successful teaching methods in helping students learn the character traits and skills is at the Class Meeting. An explanation of how to use this technique and specific meeting topics are provided in the series. At the conclusion of each meeting, students may write their reflections and thoughts about the topics on the Class Meeting form provided. These forms can be stored in students' Character Builder Notebooks.

People need responsibility. They resist assuming it, but they cannot get along without it.
—John Steinbeck

Thought for the Day. Each activity in the series is accompanied by a quote or proverb. A Thought for the Day form is provided to photocopy for students. These thoughts can also be announced over the PA speaker by a student announcer or written each morning on the blackboard. Consider having students copy the thought each day on the form and then store them in their Character Builder Notebooks. This is a great way to integrate the character trait into the literacy curriculum (reading, speaking, writing or listening).

Literature. Each *Character Builders* manual provides dozens of literature selections that can be used to highlight the value of learning the theme. Many teachers use literature as the way to define the trait to students. Choose an appropriate selection and as it is read, ask, "How did the characters demonstrate the Character Builder in the book?" "What effect did their behavior have on the other characters?" or "How did the other characters feel when the character acted . . . " (name the trait).

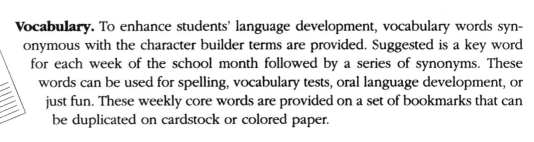

Vocabulary. To enhance students' language development, vocabulary words synonymous with the character builder terms are provided. Suggested is a key word for each week of the school month followed by a series of synonyms. These words can be used for spelling, vocabulary tests, oral language development, or just fun. These weekly core words are provided on a set of bookmarks that can be duplicated on cardstock or colored paper.

Character Builder Puppets. Each character builder theme—Responsibility, Respect, Cooperation, Peaceability, and Caring—comes with a delightful puppet designed to bring the theme to a concrete level for younger students. The puppet can be duplicated on bright-colored construction paper and attached to a ruler or paper towel tube to instantly liven up these lessons. Puppet stories to make the character traits memorable to young minds accompany some of the activities. A complete description of how to use the puppet is provided in Chapter 1.

Role Models. A natural way to infuse Character Builders into your social studies curriculum is to study real individuals whose lives depict the theme. Each *Character Builders* manual lists several possibilities of current or historical role models who demonstrate the trait. The activity can also serve as a valuable lesson as to the need for the trait.

News Articles. Ask students to collect current news articles of real people demonstating the trait. You might begin each day with a brief review of a real event in the world in which the trait was displayed. Simply take a moment to confirm the trait's value and then hang it in a space devoted to news articles about the targeted trait.

FINAL THOUGHTS

*The chains of habit are too weak to be felt until
they are too strong to be broken.*
—Dr. Johnson

Social skills and character traits are most often acquired from watching others do them right. This very premise explains why so many of today's youth are underdeveloped in these traits and skills. With the breakdown of appropriate role models for today's students, it is imperative that educators deliberately exaggerate modeling the character trait and its behaviors at the school site. This is one of the easiest and certainly most important ways to show students the behaviors of character traits and skills. Never forget your own impact on your students. You may well be the only role model a student has to "see" what a Character Builder looks and sounds like.

Dozens of activities and ideas are suggested in this manual as ways for students to practice the skills for each Character Builder trait. Additional practice opportunities are provided by activities in *Esteem Builders: A K-8 Curriculum for Improving Student Achievement, Behavior and School Climate*. And, finally, further activities are offered for parents to reinforce the skills you present in the classroom in *Home Esteem Builders*.

The program is best when it is not a "tack on" new approach but instead infuses the skills and traits into the current curriculum. Before starting a new Character Builder theme, search through your textbooks and book shelves for activities that naturally enhance the theme. Consider subjects such as literature, history, writing, art, science, math, physical education,

"Teach a child to choose the right path, and when he is older he will remain upon it."

—The Bible

music . . . every Character Builder has an endless potential of being integrated into your grade-level content. The theme will be not only more manageable for you but more meaningful for your students.

You will notice that while some of your students seem to understand the trait instantly, others need much more repetition and structured practice before they acquire the trait. If you notice some of your students have not grasped the concept, consider a few of these options:

Remodel the Trait. Many students need to "see" the trait and skills again (and again) in order to fully grasp the concept. One, two, or even three times may not be enough. Consider repeating your demonstration lesson with another student and then recreating a new T-chart with students who seem to need additional practice.

Trait Homework. Many teachers involve the parents as partners in character building. Students are required not only to practice the skills and traits at school but also at home. The more practice (particularly in a safe and supportive environment) the greater the likelihood the student will acquire the skill.

"Permanent" Safe Partners. Consider providing students who need additional practice with a "permanent" partner who is not a classmate. The term "permanent" means for a longer duration. The length of such a partnership is up to your discretion but do recognize that students low in security and in social skills are more threatened by demonstrating the trait with a number of different partners. They can benefit from having a "safer" partner they feel more secure with over a longer time period. Safe partners might include a younger student at the school (for example, a student in the sixth grade will find practicing the skill with a second grader or even kindergartener safer than a same-age partner), or a volunteer (a college or high school student or a parent).

Suppose a visitor comes to your site for the first time. He randomly pulls a student aside and asks one question: "What does your teacher or school stand for?" or "What does your teacher think are important kinds of behaviors to do?" Would the student be able to verbalize the Character Builder as an important part of your site? The answer to this question can quickly assess just how successful you've been in teaching Character Builders to your students. If that student can describe the Character Builder, it means you've accentuated the trait well enough that your students can say it to others. Keep on reinforcing it. They'll "own" it soon, which will impact their lives now and forever.

"You can easily judge the character of a man by how he treats those who can do nothing for him."

—James D. Miles

 1

How to Build Character

How to Build Character

respect vb. to consider worthy of high regard.

esteem n 1. the quality or state of being esteemed; honor.

2. expression of respect or deference.

have the opportunity of working with hundreds of teachers each year in my seminars. Two years ago I decided to start conducting an informal poll with my participants. I asked them one simple question: "What one trait or skill to you think today's students need that would help them be more successful in school and in life?" Hands down in every group to which I've presented teachers vote unanimously for respect. Teachers feel a majority of today's students are lacking this essential character builder (responsibility running a close second) and as a result are much more difficult to deal with in a classroom. Disrespect, negativity, lack of consideration, poor manners, and low esteem are all behavioral outcomes. Why? The premise is simple but powerful: If you don't have respect for who you are, it's next to impossible for children to have respect for others.

Respect is one of the most desirable character builders. When children possess this character trait they are more likely to care about the rights of others. These students are more pleasant to have in a classroom because they're able to think about other persons in a more positive, caring way. Because these children care about the feelings of others, they show respect for themselves, too. You'll hear these students saying more positive self-statements and evaluating their performance more realistically as well as taking care of their body and health. These children treat others the way they want to be treated. And perhaps therein lies the greatest reason respect is dying as a strong character trait in today's children: far too many of our students have been treated disrespectfully in their homes and by their peers. Far too many of our children are being exposed to a preponderance of sarcastic, disrespectful, negative statements. And far too many of our students are viewing an overwhelming number of scenes on the media that not only portray disrespect but also undermine human dignity.

It has become increasingly difficult for many of our students to "catch respectful attitudes" because the trait seems to be on a decline worldwide. When tuning into the news, notice how many top stories these days deal with disrespect. In this decade, we've watched in horror scenes of children engaged in horrific disrespectful acts: a junior high student from Japan confesses to the beheading of a younger student; a high school senior from the United States, afraid of missing her prom, gives birth and then allegedly strangles her baby so she won't miss the next dance; an elementary-aged boy from England beats a young child to death. And the scenes continue each day in the news. The epitome of disrespect is a complete disrespect for human life.

A general decline in respect for self also pervades our cities and streets. A rise in teenage suicide and alchohol and substance abuse haunts parents and teachers alike. These trends will continue to escalate unless we make a full-scale emergency intervention to stop them.

If the breakdown of this trait in today's youth is as widesread as the news reports depict it, we need to do everything we can to rebuild it in our students. Respect is simply not being modeled nearly enough for students to understand not only its meaning and value, but also its basic characteristics—what it looks and sounds like. Respect is a character builder that extends far beyond the classroom. This is a trait vital for developing solid citizenship and decent interpersonal relationships. This is a trait vital for success in school as well as in life. If we want our students to acquire this critical character builder, we need to intentionally teach them the behaviors of respect. And that's the good news: respect is a trait that can be taught. This second manual in the *Character Builder* series addresses how to help students understand the meaning and value of respect as well as learn the skills of respect so they can display them on their own without our prompting and reinforcement.

Remember, the only place your students may ever see the demonstration of this critical character builder is by watching you...so intentially tune up the trait in your behavior and accentuate the value of respect.

Educators can aid students in developing the trait of respect by taking the following steps:

Steps to Building Respect

1. Teach the meaning and value of respect.

2. Create a respectful learning environment.

3. Enhance respect towards others.

4. Teach how to listen respectfully.

This manual provides you with practical, research-based activities to teach students this essential character builder. The learning outcomes for your students will be ones they will use not only now but for the rest of their lives. Here are some of the lifetime benefits your students will acquire from using the lessons in *Respect*:

Respect Learning Outcomes

- Create a learning environment where students are free from humiliation, ridicule or put-downs.

- Develop a feeling of emotional safety in a caring and respectful learning environment.

- Recognize and use the language of respect.

- Learn to respect one's self and consider the rights of others.

- Accentuate respect and eliminate disrespect.

- Develop the skill of sending and receiving respectful compliments.

- Practice respectful listening behaviors and understand how listening builds respect.

RESPECT SKILL BUILDERS

Receiving Compliments (RS28)

BE RESPECTFUL · BE COURTEOUS · LISTEN · SHARE · ADMIRE · BE CONSIDERATE

RECEIVING COMPLIMENTS

4 Steps to Receiving a Compliment

1. Look at the sender.
2. Hold your head high.
3. Use a clear voice.
4. Say "thank you" like you mean it.

"Thanks for noticing."   "That made me feel good."

"Thank you."   "I value your opinion."

"I'm grateful."   "When you say that I feel good."

"I appreciate it when you..." "I really like it when you..."

"I appreciate that."   "Thanks!"

THAT'S A GREAT HAIR CUT!

THANK YOU.

BE COMPLIMENTARY · LISTEN · BE CONSIDERATE · BE POLITE · BE COURTEOUS

I Like Messages (RS28).

Sending Compliments (RS22).

Respectful Messages (RS14b).

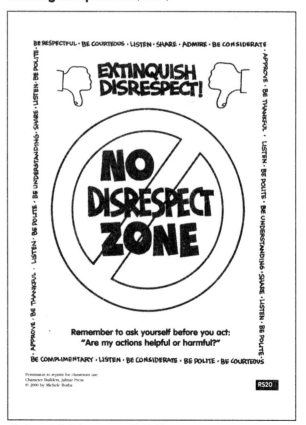

Extinquish Disrespect (RS20).

"True politeness is perfect ease in freedom. It simply consists in treating others just as you love to be treated yourself.

—Earl of Chester-field

Respect Vocabulary

Week 1: Respect

Week 2: Honest

Week 3: Decent

Week 4. Reputation

Models of Respect

Dan Jansen	Big Bird	Lee Iacocca
Matt Biondi	Norman Vincent Peale	The Pioneers
Barney	Bonnie Blair	Neil Armstrong
Mr. Rogers	Anne Frank	Eleanor Roosevelt
Martin Luther King, Jr.	Albert Schweitzer	Jacques Cousteau
John Muir	Mahatma Ghandi	Thomas Edison
Michael Jordan	Nelson Mandela	Abraham Lincoln
Desmond Tutu		

Respect Theme Song: R-E-S-P-E-C-T by Aretha Franklin

Respect Motto: "Give respect to get respect."

STEPS TO BUILDING CHARACTER TRAITS

Though each of the five Character Builders in this program are unique and consist of distinct skills and behaviors, the steps to teaching each character trait (Responsibility, Respect, Cooperation, Peaceability, and Caring) are the same. The staff should utilize the same five steps in teaching each Character Builder in this series. Skipping any step will be detrimental to the students' acquisition of the concept. There's an old Chinese proverb which is quite appropriate to the learning process. It says: "If you cut too many corners, you end up going around in circles." Each step is important in helping students learn these five core Character Builders.

Character Skill Builder Teaching Steps

1. **TARGET:** Focus on the Character Builder for at least 21 days.

2. **DEFINE:** Describe the need, value, and meaning of the trait.

3. **SHOW:** Teach what the trait looks like and sounds like.

4. **DO:** Provide structured practice of the trait for 21 days.

5. **REINFORCE:** Give immediate feedback and encourage use in life.

STEP 1: TARGET
Focus on the Character Builder

The first step to teaching any new character trait, skill or behavior is to target the skill visually (and ideally orally) to students. The more students "see" the trait the more they recognize that "these must be important...there they are again." If Character Builders are being accentuated school-wide, it is important that the poster for each theme and skill be accentuated throughout the school site. Everyone at the school needs to be reminded of the theme.

Quick Ways to Target a Character Builder

- Clearly announce to students what the targeted trait is and keep it posted.

- Keep the Character Builder trait or skill posted as long as possible. Many teachers add a new Character Builder poster to their walls every month or two.

- Tell students your expectations regarding the trait.

- Announce the trait over the loudspeaker or at least start each morning with a one-minute Character Builder announcement.

- If Character Builders are being accentuated school-wide, it is important that the poster for each theme and skill be accentuated throughout the school site. Everyone at the school needs to be reminded of the theme.

Keeping the Focus on Character

There are dozens of ways to focus on character traits and skills. Below are listed some of the simplest as well as some of the most unique ways to accentuate a character trait.

- **Character Builder Poster.** Each Character Builder trait comes with an 8½" × 11" poster. Photocopy the poster on bright-colored paper and hang it on walls for all to see. The form in this book can be enlarged at a printer's to a 18" × 24" size. The Character Builder puppet can be enlarged to hang up as a visual reminder for younger children.

- **Character Builder Assembly.** Many sites implementing school-wide character themes introduce the trait at a school-wide assembly. At this occasion the staff describes why the trait is important, distributes the poster to students, and even presents a short skit or movie about the trait.

- **Screen Saver.** This one wins the prize for the "most unique way to accentuate a character trait." I saw it at a magnet school in computers and technology. Each day a staff or student member wrote a brief sentence describing a school rule, theme or learning message about the targeted Character Builder on the site's central screen saver. Whenever anyone at the school used a computer, the first thing they saw was the screen saver message accentuating the trait.

- **Campaign Posters.** Student-made posters are often the simplest way to accentuate a character trait. Students can draw the guidelines using material such as colored poster board, marking pens, and construction paper. Posters can also be computer-generated and printed on colored paper. However posters are made, be sure to hang them everywhere and anywhere on school and classroom walls.

- **Flag Pole Banner.** On visiting a middle school in Austin, Texas, I knew when I was in the parking lot what behaviors that staff was accentuating for their students. A banner made from an old white sheet hung on the flag pole. Imprinted with bold-colored permanent marking, the banner stated one word: "EFFORT!" Each month the staff selected a different trait, and a group of students volunteered to make and hang the banner.

- **Character Builder Announcements.** By using the school loud speaker system, students can be orally reminded of the character traits and skills. Many schools use the first and last minute of each school day for Character Builder reminders. Principals can announce names of students "caught demonstrating the trait." Students can describe ways to appropriately demonstrate the traits or behaviors.

- **Character Builder Theme Songs.** A unique way to accentuate each Character Builder is by selecting a "theme song" to match each character trait. Play it over the loud speaker before the bell rings and during lunch. For example, the song from the television show, "Cheers," is a great way to accentuate the theme of Cooperation. There is no better song for the theme of Respect than Aretha Franklin's tune by the same name, "Respect."

> "Whoever one is, and wherever one is, one is always in the wrong if one is rude."
>
> —Maurice Baring

STEP 2: DEFINE

Describe the Need, Value and Meaning of the Trait

The second step to teaching a new character trait or behavior is to convey to students exactly what the trait means and why it is important to learn. Though the trait may be targeted in the classroom and on dozens of posters throughout the campus, never assume students understand what the trait means. The trait should always be explained to students so that they can understand the concept within their knowledge base and experience. Though each Character Builder poster has a carefully constructed definition, keep in mind a definition generated by the students will be even more powerful. Here are a few other ways to define new traits and behaviors to students.

Quick Ways to Define a Character Builder

- Tell students specifically why they should learn the skill.

- Clearly explain the value of learning the trait.

- Specifically define the trait to students. "This is what I mean when I say the word caring…."

- Keep the definition posted in your classroom and, ideally, all around the school.

- Use your own personal examples to make the definition concrete.

- Find literature selections that define the trait.

- Ask students to clip news articles of events or people demonstrating the theme.

Below are many powerful suggestions of specific ways you can define a Character Builder for your students:

- **Define in Teachable Moments.** Use teachable moments to accentuate, define and model new behaviors to students. You might accentuate the behavior of "encouragement" by patting a student on the back and saying: "Keep it up. I know you can do it!" Take one more second to label and define the trait by saying, "Did you notice I just encouraged you?" Finally, define the behavior to the student in context by adding "…because I just patted you on the back and told you I knew you could do it." Many students need a moment to process the concept in context.

- **Label Traits as Students Use Them.** Whenever you see or hear a student displaying the targeted trait, take a moment to label it to the rest of the students. Point out specifically what the student did that demonstrated the trait and remember to be consistent in the use of terms. For instance, if "respect" is the term that appears on the Character Builder poster, use this same term to reinforce a student's behavior. Here are the steps to labeling a new behavior.

1. First, point out the behavior as soon as convenient with a label.

It is always best to point out the behavior the moment it happens so the student will be more likely to recall what he or she did. Also, any other students who are near the reinforced student will also benefit from hearing "what was done right." Suppose you are reinforcing "respect." Stop and label the appropriate behavior to the student:

"Alex, that was respectful…"

> *"Good manners and soft words have brought many a difficult thing to pass."*
>
> —Sir John Vanbrugh

2. *Second, tell the student specifically what they did that was appropriate.*

Usually, you can begin with the word "because" and then confirm to the student exactly what he or she did that was "respectful."

> "…because you waited until I was finished
> talking before you spoke."

- **Tell the Trait's Benefits.** Skills and behaviors are more meaningful and relevant to students if they understand the benefit of learning the skill. Take a moment to say the name of the Character Builder or the skill and why it's important. For example, "This month we will be learning about the value of caring. It's such an important trait because it helps make the world a kinder and gentler place."

- **Share Personal Beliefs.** Students need to hear your convictions regarding the trait. Why do you personally feel the trait is important? If you are targeting the trait of "respect," you might tell students how adamant you feel about not talking negatively about yourself or others. For instance, you could say: "One of the things that bothers me most is when I hear someone saying something unkind about themselves or someone else. I know unkindness hurts. In this classroom it is not allowed." Show them with your own behavior how strongly you believe in what you say.

- **Student Reporters.** One of the easiest ways to demonstrate the need for the trait is to point out its value in context. Anytime someone displays the trait, take a moment to label the Character Builder to students. Suppose you are accentuating "caring." Ask students to begin looking for others demonstrating the trait at the school. These students can assume the role of "reporters." Their job is to report back to the class who demonstrated the trait, what the student did, and most important, the effect the student's actions had on another individual. The sequence might sound like this:

> "Politeness is not always the sign of wisdom, but the want of it always leaves room for the suspicion of folly."
> —Walter Savage Landor

TEACHER:	Did anyone see someone who was caring today?
JOHN:	I did. I saw Jennifer being caring.
TEACHER:	What did you see Jennifer do that was caring?
JOHN:	I saw her help another student who fell down. She went to the nurse's office to get a Band-Aid and get help.
TEACHER:	That was caring. Did you notice how the hurt student felt after Jennifer helped her?
JOHN:	Well, at first the student was crying really hard. Jennifer kept talking quietly to her and pretty soon the girl stopped crying.
TEACHER:	How do you think the girl felt when Jennifer showed she cared about her?
JOHN:	I think she felt better inside.

The dialogue between the teacher and John may have taken no more than a minute, but it was a powerful exchange. The teacher verified not only to John but also to the other students the kind of positive effect caring can have on others. The simple conversation became a significant lesson highlighting the need for learning caring.

STEP 3: SHOW
Teach What the Trait Looks Like and Sounds Like

Now comes the moment when you teach the Character Builder to your students. Very often the prior steps (targeting and defining) are skipped. As a result, many students fail to learn the skills so critical to the trait. There is no perfect way to teach the trait. A few suggested techniques that have been field-tested and proven successful are offered. The most important part of effective teaching is to try and make the trait as "hands on" and meaningful as possible. Never assume students have the language or cognitive acquisition of the trait. Many do not. You can make a significant difference in your students' lives (both now and in the future!) by modeling the trait yourself and making your Character Builder lessons as concrete as possible.

Quick Ways to Show a Character Builder

- Model the trait showing specific behaviors.

- Another staff member can model the trait with you to the class in a quick role play.

- Send a videocamera crew of students on a search for other students modeling the trait. Capture the Character Builder trait on video and then play it for everyone else to see.

- Create, with students, a T-Chart of the skill/trait and, as you develop the chart, model what it looks like and sounds like.

- Identify famous individuals who emulate the skill/trait. Ask students to read biographies about their lives and/or report what the individual specifically did to demonstrate the skill.

- Photograph students demonstrating the trait and make a chart students can refer to.

Role Playing

One of the best ways to teach behaviors or traits is by role playing what it looks like to students. This need not take more than 30 seconds (honestly!), but it is a step that should not be skipped. Your students need to know exactly what the trait looks and sounds like. Role playing can be adapted for younger children by having them play out Character Builder behaviors using the puppets. Suppose you want to teach students the behavior of attentive listening. Here are the steps you could use to model the trait:

1. Begin by choosing a confident student or another staff member to help you role play the trait. The two of you should stand in a location so that all of your students can see your behavior (the other person in the role play is not who the students are to watch—it's you!) Tell students: "In the next minute you'll have the opportunity to watch what listening looks and sounds like. Watch me carefully. I'm going to show (name of the other person) that I'm listening to her."

2. Tell the other person to relax and think of anything he did before coming to school that day that he would like to share. Explain that he can say anything and that if he runs out of things to say he is allowed to make things up. You might have another student time you so that the activity does not extend beyond 30 seconds.

3. As the other person begins talking, your role is to demonstrate to the group what the Character Builder skill (in this instance, "attentive listening") looks like. Turn the participant towards you so that the two of you are standing face to face and sideways to the group so that the class sees only your outside shoulders. Once the student begins speaking, deliberately don't say anything except "uh huh" or "yes." Your job is to convey good listening behaviors such as facing your partner squarely at all times, not interrupting, raising your eyebrows at key points, smiling and nodding, appearing animated or enthused, leaning forward slightly, looking directly into the speaker's eyes, and keeping your arms at your sides. At the end of the minute, thank the participant and tell the class to give the person a big hand.

4. On the blackboard, transparency or chart paper draw a large T-chart that covers the full space of the medium you are working with. Write the name of the Character Builder trait or skill at the top of the board. To the left, write "Looks Like" and to the right side "Sounds Like." Now create a T-Chart such as the one below:

Attentive Listening

Looks Like	Sounds Like

> "Rudeness is the weak man's imitation of strength."
>
> —Eric Hoffer

5. Tell students you just showed them what the skill of "attentive listening" looks and sounds like. Now ask them to specify what they saw you do that showed them you were attentively listening to the participant. Remind students of the rules for brainstorming. You may want to post the Brainstorming Rules Poster from "Responsibility" book (RT13a) near the chart to remind students of the rules. Emphasize that "no put downs are allowed."

6. For younger students, images of an eye for "Looks Like" and an ear for "Sounds Like" are included in each manual to duplicate, cut out and tape to the T-chart. Say, "Remember, I want you to tell me first only what you saw me do. What you saw me do is called 'Looks Like.'" List the group's ideas under the "Looks Like" side of the chart. Continually remind the group to be very specific. Write the concrete list of words or phrases students generate in the discussion. If students have difficulty recalling listening behaviors, you might wish to remind them by modeling the behavior with your body. For example, to help students recall that your body was

facing square to the student, you might ask: "Where was my body facing? Where were my shoulders? Were they here (turn your shoulders away from the student) or were they here?" (Turn your shoulders square to the student.) When a list has been obtained, ask the group to now refer to the "Sounds Like" side of the chart.

A completed group chart might look like this:

> "There can be no defense like elaborate courtesy."
>
> —E.V. Lucas

Attentive Listening

Looks Like	Sounds Like
nodding	Yes.
smiling	Uh huh.
eye to eye	Ahhh.
leaning in	That's interesting.
face to face	Really?
raised eyebrows	Thanks!
feet flat	Then what?
hands in lap	What next?

7. Emphasize to the students that you deliberately did not say much during the activity other than "uh huh" and "yes." The first step to attentive listening is making sure your body is sending messages that show you are listening.

8. Mention that the kinds of things we can say to demonstrate we are listening can be taught at a later time and will be added to the list. You might ask the group for a few phrases or words a student could say to another student to let the person know he or she is listening. These could be included under "Sounds Like," such as: "Yes," "That's interesting," "Really?," "I didn't know that," "Thanks!," "Then what?" and "What next?"

It is important to create a T-chart of behaviors for each Character Builder trait you teach to students, and it is always more meaningful for students to create their own charts rather than be provided with one "pre-made." A T-chart form in Character Builders is provided for students to fill out and keep in their Character Builder Notebooks following each lesson.

The completed T-chart should then be hung in the classroom as a visual reminder of the trait or the behavior. New words and behaviors should continue to be added to the chart throughout the year as students recognize additional Character Building behaviors.

Chart Variations for Younger Students

- **Photographs.** Capture students actually displaying the Character Builder behaviors on film. Develop the pictures, enlarge them slightly on a copying machine and paste them on a chart labeling the trait.

- **Butcher Paper.** Ask a student to lay down on a piece of long butcher paper and trace around their body outline. Hang up the paper and ask students to now show what different parts of the body do to show the speaker the Character Builder trait. Print these behaviors inside the outline next to the body part. For "listening," for instance, a chart might include: mouth closed, hands in lap, feet flat on the floor, head nodding, eyes on speaker.

STEP 4: DO
Provide Structured Practice of the Trait

Showing students what the Character Builder looks and sounds like is not enough. In most cases, students must be provided with frequent structured opportunities to practice the new behaviors. In fact, behavior management theory tells us it generally takes 21 days of repetition or practice before a new behavior is acquired. This is an important rule to keep in mind as you try these activities with your students. You will see change if you continue to model the behavior, provide consistent opportunities for students to practice the skill, and reinforce appropriate behaviors. One of the greatest benefits of Character Builders is the program is designed to be used for a minimum of 21 days.

Quick Ways to Practice a Character Builder

- Allow students at least 21 days to practice the skill in frequent structured opportunities.
- Practice sessions can be done in "learning buddies" or "base teams."
- Role play the skill/trait. Younger students can role play Character Builder behaviors using the puppet.
- Students can keep a "reflection log" of their behavior progress with the trait.
- Use any teachable moments to ask: "Is that a stopper or a starter?"
- Character Builder "homework" can be assigned by requiring students to practice the skill at home with their family.

STEP 5: REINFORCE
Give Immediate Feedback and Encourage Use in Life

The final step to teaching a Character Builder is to reinforce students' appropriate behavior or correct inappropriate behavior as soon as it is convenient to do so and encourage them to use the trait in their own lives. There are two important reasons to reinforce the Character Builder trait or skill:

1. It helps clarify to the student that he/she is on the right track and that he/she should keep up the good work. The student immediately recognizes the demonstrated trait because you pointed it out on the spot. Behavior management theory says the student is more likely to repeat the behavior again because he knows what he did right.

2. The reinforced student serves as a model to any other students who happened to be nearby the moment the student was recognized. Keep in mind most social skills are learned through watching others. The frustrating part of teaching for many educators has been the simple fact that appropriate role models are breaking down for our students. Anytime we can use a peer as an appropriate role model and specifically let other students know what the student did that was correct, we are helping those students learn the appropriate behavior.

Quick Ways to Reinforce a Character Builder

- Give specific feedback ASAP: students did the trait right or wrong.

- Tell students exactly what they did right or wrong. If they were correct, say what they did right. If the behavior was wrong, say what they can do next time. Waiting until the end of the day is too late. With some kids, waiting five minutes later is too late. Students benefit from immediate correction.

- Redo the behavior with students on the spot by pointing out or showing exactly what the students should do to replace the incorrect behavior pattern.

- Give students "constructive criticism." Tell what was wrong. Tell what to do to make it right. Be brief. Be private. Be specific and remember: emphasize only the student's behavior, never their character.

- Reinforce to students whenever the skill is done correctly. Use "catching the skill done correctly" as a teachable moment for the rest of the class.

- Provide students with reinforcement tickets, coupons and awards. Character Builders includes a number of these forms for each character trait and skill.

- The Character Builder puppet for each trait can be constantly used as a reinforcer for children. Look for a child who has correctly demonstrated the Character Builder and quietly place the puppet on his/her desk. This child then looks for another student demonstrating the trait and places the puppet on this person's desk. It's a silent reinforcer that tunes students into looking for appropriate behaviors.

STUDENT CHARACTER BUILDERS

One can acquire everything in solitude—except character.
—HENRI BEYLE

Students can be instrumental in helping peers (and staff) "catch a character attitude" by involving them in the planning and implementation of the Character Builder activities. Ideally, these students should be of various ages. This committee can become a core group of students for the year or can be changed monthly. If the committee is to be a school-wide group of students, one or two faculty members can become committee advisors whose job is to coordinate the student group. Possibilities for involving students are endless. Here are a few ideas other school sites have used:

"Human beings can alter their lives by altering their attitudes."

—William James

- **Student Campaign Committee.** As each new Character Builder is introduced, the Student Campaign Committee begins a blitz of creating banners, signs and posters to hang up around the school convincing the rest of the students of the merit of the theme.

- **Student Announcement Group.** Many classrooms, as well as schools, begin the day with a one-minute message "advertising" the theme. The advertisement may include a powerful quotation to think about, an announcement reinforcing students "caught" demonstrating the Character Builder or even a quick commercial stating the value of learning the theme. Teachers ask different students daily or weekly to assume this role. Administrators have students make announcements over the school PA system.

- **Skit Committee.** This group of students creates a skit or role play about the Character Builder and performs it at either a school-wide assembly or in each classroom. The skit shows other students the value of the trait as well as what the Character Builder looks and sounds like. (Idea from Lakeview School, Minneapolis.)

- **Video Crew.** If you have access to video equipment, you might consider teaching a core group of students how to use it. A student video crew could record actual students demonstrating the trait. They might also video the students' Character Builder skit. The video is then shown in each classroom.

HOW TO USE CHARACTER BUILDER PUPPETS

Developmental learning theory clearly tells us that young children learn best through concrete experiences. The Character Builder puppets in this series were designed with this concept in mind. Each book is accompanied by a puppet as well as stories, role playing and follow-up activities that present the core lessons in a meaningful and fun way.

Meet the Character Builder Puppets

Responsibility

Able

Behavior Traits: He's a star you can always count on; he's dependable, trustworthy, reliable.

RP1

Caring

Sunshine

RP5

Behavior Traits: She's a sun who brings warmth and happiness to those she touches.

Respect

Admiral

RP4

Behavior Traits: He's a moon you can look up to and admire; he's earned respect through caring actions.

Disrespect/Negativity

Stinger

RP3

Behavior Traits: He's an unhappy star who puts others down.

Cooperation

Pal and Goldie

RP6

Behavior Traits: They are planets who depend on each other; they work together to accomplish their goals.

Irresponsible

Spinner

Behavior Traits: He's a comet who has poor judgment and a quick temper; he spins out of control.

RP7

Peaceableness

Sparky

RP2

Behavior Traits: He's a star who is always positive; he sparkles and shines with builder-uppers.

Aggressive

Burner

Behavior Traits: He's a meteor who is belligerent and attacking; he burns himself out.

RP8

Note: Larger versions of the above characters can be found in the Puppets section.

The Character Builder puppets will appear periodically in each book to reinforce a lesson or concept. If they are to be used in the activity, they will be listed in the materials section. Just look for the gray tone and a small replica of the puppet. A story for younger children using the puppet to describe the Character Builder concepts is then provided.

There are many ways the puppet can be used to liven up the session and reinforce the Character Builder concepts. Here are a few ways the puppet images can be used to make the lessons concrete and memorable for young children:

- *Felt Puppet.* To make the puppet durable for years of use, trace and cut the puppet head shape provided in each manual onto felt. Glue the felt shape onto heavy cardboard and cut it out again for a stiff figure. Three dimensional features can be attached to the figure with a glue gun: buttons, movable eyes, yarn hair, pom-poms, and even sequins or rickrack. Finally, attach a wooden dowel to the back of the puppet with heavy masking tape or a glue gun to create a puppet ready to tell character building stories.

- *Paper Stick Puppet.* The easiest way to make any of the Character Builder puppets is simply to duplicate the puppet head provided in the manual onto colored construction paper or cardstock-weight paper. Cut out the shape and tape it to a paper towel tube, a ruler, or a wooden dowel. Students love making their own puppets with you.

- *Paper Bag Puppet.* Duplicate the puppet head onto colored construction paper or cardstock-weight paper, cut out the shape and glue it to the front flap of a lunch-size paper bag. Features can be added to the face or body using items such as colored paper scraps, noodles, egg carton pieces, pipe cleaners, wall paper samples, yarn, bric-a-brac, and fabric.

- *Shape Book Cover.* Duplicate the puppet shape onto light-colored construction paper or cardstock. Cut two copies along the outside margin of the shape for a front and back book cover along with several pieces of writing paper so that the cover and writing paper are the same size. Place the writing pages inside the front and back cover and staple the pages along the top or sides. The book may now be used by students to write, draw, dictate further adventure stories about the characters, or describe what they learned in the lesson.

- *Award.* Duplicate the puppet head on cardstock or light-colored construction paper and cut out the shape. Punch two holes along the top, string a long 36" piece of yarn through the holes and tie the ends into a knot. The shape can be hung from the neck of any student who demonstrates the Character Builder trait or behavior.

- *Hats.* Fun hats for students to wear while role playing the stories are easy to make. Here are two quick versions:

  1. Fold up the opening on a medium-size grocery bag about two inches. Duplicate a copy of the shape on colored construction paper or cardstock, cut it out and glue or staple it to the front. The student puts the bag on his head for a hat.

  2. Duplicate a copy of the puppet shape on colored construction paper or cardstock and cut it out. Cut a strip of tagboard or construction paper 3" × 28", bring the ends together so they overlap about two inches and staple them. Finally staple the puppet head shape to the front of the strip to wear as a hat.

- *Puppet Bag.* Copy the puppet head shape onto paper and cut it out along the outside edge. Glue or staple the head to the front of a lunch-size brown bag. The opened bag sits on top of students' desks. Use the puppet bags to send notes of encouragement (from you and the students) or to congratulate one another on demonstrating the character trait symbolized by the puppet.

- *Starter and Stopper Puppets.* To help students reflect on appropriate and inappropriate language and behaviors for each of the Character Builder traits, two traffic shapes are included for role playing and storytelling. The Go Sign (page RT2d) signifies "starter" language and behaviors, or the kinds of things people who demonstrate the character trait would say and do. The Stop Sign (page RT2e) represents "stopper" language and behaviors or inappropriate words and actions that do not depict the character trait. The stopper sign is duplicated on red construction paper or cardstock and cut out; the starter sign on green. The signs can easily be made into puppets by gluing, taping or stapling a paper towel tube, ruler or wooden dowel to the back of the shape. The stick is now ready for role playing. The shapes can also be glued to charts, pinned to bulletin boards or taped on a blackboard to enhance a lesson using the concept.

> "I com-
> plained
> because I
> had no
> shoes until
> I met a
> man who
> had no
> feet."
>
> —Arabic
> Proverb

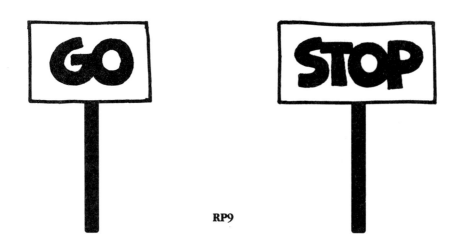

RP9

- *Looks Like/Sounds Like Puppets.* To help students recognize the kinds of things people who demonstrate the character trait say and do, two shapes—an ear and an eye—are included in the manual. The ear and eye shapes are duplicated on construction paper and cut out. The shapes can then be glued, taped or stapled to a paper towel tube, ruler or wooden dowel for a stick puppet to use in role playing. The shapes can also be glued to charts, pinned to bulletin boards or taped on a blackboard to enhance a lesson using the concept.

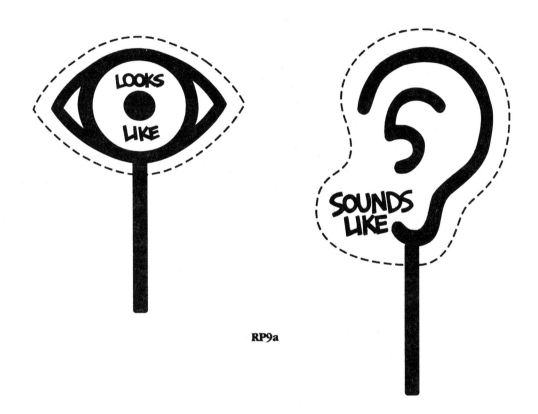

RP9a

The concrete activities provided in this manual as well as the other four supporting books in this series offer endless possibilities for building the essential character traits in your students. Remember, to help students learn these new skills for now, as well as for the rest of their lives, keep the five steps to enhancing Character Builder skills in mind:

1. **TARGET:** Focus on the Character Builder for at least 21 days.

2. **DEFINE:** Describe the need, value and meaning of the trait.

3. **SHOW:** Teach what the trait looks like and sounds like.

4. **DO:** Provide structured practice of the trait for 21 days.

5. **REINFORCE:** Give immediate feedback and encourage use in life.

 2

Teaching Respect

KEY CONCEPTS

- Recognizing and using the language of respect.
- Learning to respect self.
- Considering the rights of others.
- Earning respect through showing respect.

2

Teaching Respect

*People seldom improve when they have
no model to copy but themselves.*
—ANONYMOUS

Like responsibility, respect is not something you give to a child. They must learn it and earn it themselves. The first step to helping students learn the character trait of respect is to teach them why it is valuable and what it means. As you plan your lessons keep this rule in mind: Don't assume students have any understanding about the trait. Many of the character traits and skills that we take for granted everyone should know are rapidly dying in our youth. Their exposure to these character builders are oftentimes limited. The significant models in their lives may not ever have acquired the traits themselves, thus their opportunities to practice the skills that nurture the character builders are dramatically reduced. In too many cases, the school may well be the only place today's youth can experience these behaviors.

CHARACTER BUILDER STEP #1

Teach the Meaning and Value of Respect

The most significant way to help students learn this core character builder is by treating them respectfully. Keep in mind that the classroom may well be the only place during the day where students can experience what respect looks and sounds like. The activities in this first section are designed to help students understand the meaning and value of the character builder trait of respect.

> "My feeling is that there is nothing in life but refraining from hurting others, and comforting those that are sad."
> — Oliver Schreiner

To find out more about the second building block of self-esteem, Selfhood, and how it impacts teaching the character builder of respect, the following resources are recommended:

Resources to Enhance Student Respect

The activities listed below are taken from the *Esteem Builders* series written by Dr. Michele Borba.

Source   **Page**

To enhance an awareness of Selfhood, the esteem component for Respect.

Trainer's Manual:
Staff Development Training Session 2:
    "A Strong Foundation: Building Security"   117-124

Audiocassette 2:
Building Blocks of Self-Esteem:
    "A Strong Foundation: Building Selfhood"

WHAT IS RESPECT?   RS 1

Purpose: To help students understand the meaning of respect. To teach students what the behavior of respect "looks like" and "sounds like."

Thought: *True politeness is perfect ease in freedom. It simply consists in treating others just as you love to be treated yourself.*—Earl of Chesterfield

Materials:
- Respect Poster (RS1a); one per student and one enlarged poster size.
- Character Builder Notebook (RS1c).

For older students
- Looks Like/Sounds Like (RS1d); one per student.
- How I Feel (RT1e)

For younger students:
- Admiral the Moon Puppet (RS1b).
- Eye/Ear/Heart Images (RS1f, RT1g, RT1h); one copy duplicated and cut out.

Procedure: To create the hand puppet: Cut out two identical puppet shapes from the original pattern. Ideally, you want to cut the shapes out of heavy, non-fraying fabric such as felt. Hand or machine stitch the two shapes together 1/4" from the edges, leaving at least 6" open at the bottom for a hand to fit through. The material can also be attached using a glue gun.

A less durable hand puppet can be made from two pieces of heavy paper, though it may be difficult to bend the shape when the puppet is acting in the scenes. When using material other than felt, cut the puppet at least 1/2" larger than the original pattern. Turn the two pieces right sides facing together and then machine or hand stitch 1/4" from the outside edge.

Now turn the two sewn pieces cut from material or heavy paper inside out. The puppet is ready to be decorated with movable eyes, yarn hair, a yarn or felt mouth, or any other features of your choice.

To begin the activity: Write the term "respect" on a chart or the board and ask for meanings from students. Responses might include: treating people nicely, showing courtesy to others, letting others feel you value them, making others feel good, listening to other people's ideas, caring about the rights of others, thinking about another person in a positive way, showing consideration for yourself and others, treating property nicely, admiring another person's special skills or strengths, looking up to someone. Introduce the theme poster: Respect (RS1a).

Define the term "respect" as "valuing someone or something. To show respect means you treat others in a courteous, polite manner. When you treat other people the same way you'd like to be treated, you respect them and are showing you value them." Explain that for the next few weeks of school, students will be learning what respect is and why this trait is important to help them succeed. Tell them they will also learn how they can show respect for one another to make the classroom a more friendly and positive place.

To make the idea of respect concrete, you could use an analogy. Say: "Respect is like the moon. We look up at the moon and admire its size, shape and natural beauty. We value the moon because it's the earth's only satellite and our greatest source of light at night. Even though it is more than 238,000 miles away, it's our closest neighbor in the universe. Before we had clocks, we kept track of the passing of days by looking up at the moon. A lunar cycle is roughly 28 days or one month, and twelve of these cycles represents one year. To record the passage of time is just one of many reasons the moon has value for people."

How Admiral Earned His Respect

For younger students, use Admiral the Moon Puppet to continue telling the story. "Admiral is the name of a moon. His name comes from the word admire. What does admire mean?" Wait for responses such as "look up to, think highly of, want to be like, consider valuable and worthwhile." Point out that "admire" means the same as the word "respect." Tell students the story of how Admiral the Moon earned his respect.

"Long time ago when people used to worship the sun, the moon hid itself because it didn't think it could ever be as good and admired as the sun. During this time when there were shrines and monuments built to the sun, the moon considered itself just a pale reflection of the much larger and brighter light of the sun.

"For many years the sun would come up in the morning and throw its strong light across the earth. And as its light grew warmer and more brilliant the sun would shake its head in discouragement because he could see that all had not gone well the night before. There were travelers who had gotten lost at night, and crops that hadn't been planted on time because farmers had lost track of the seasons. There were people leaving litter on the ground and work unfinished because they ran out of daylight. The sun decided it was time for the moon to come out of hiding.

"Not everyone knows this, but the moon is actually very shy. Sunshine, that's the name of the sun, coaxed the moon out of the shadows by shining its light a little more warmly than usual. Then she spoke some kind words to ease his fears. 'Your light may not be as strong as mine, but you'd be amazed at what a difference just a little bit of light would make at night. Here, I'll help you out." Then the sun directed a soft beam of light onto the face of the moon which bounced back and struck the earth. The moon felt uncomfortable being in the spotlight. He drew up his shoulders and turned his body to the side, which appeared as a thin crescent shape in the sky. The moon wanted to know what it was supposed to do with this light. 'Just look around and you'll see,' Sunshine said.

"The first place the moon looked was in a forest where a caravan of travelers had stopped to set up camp for the night. They were barbecuing meat and throwing the bones all over the ground. The moon shone his light on the spot and when the people saw what a mess they had made they began to clean up all their litter. Without saying a word, the moon had taught them to have respect for their environment. Then with a full moon overhead, the travelers decided to continue part of their journey at night in order to avoid the scorching heat of the day.

"Next the moon found some farm workers who were exhausted from working all day in the cornfields. After the moon shone on them, the workers realized they could do some of their work at night when it was cool and take a nap during the hottest part of the day. So that's what they did. During the day they reaped their crops and at night they shucked corn and shared laughter and good times together. They even put up a scarecrow so the crows would think a human was in the fields twenty-four hours a day and not bother the crops before they had a chance to mature. The owner of the cornfield also began to respect the land and the cycles of nature when he learned to plant his crops by the spring equinox.

"Finally the moon's big all-seeing eye noticed a brother and sister who refused to go to bed when they were supposed to. They argued with their parents, saying they couldn't go to sleep without keeping a candle burning all night. After listening to both sides of the argument, the moon decided to help out by shining a soft beam of light through their bedroom window. After that, the children had no more problems falling asleep at night. And when they went to bed on time they discovered they could get up earlier in the morning. The children learned to respect their parents as well as the always watchful eye of the moon.

"From that time until now the moon came to be known as Admiral, someone worthy of receiving our admiration and respect, because he made a difference in the lives of so many people. Admiral earned his respect by doing kind deeds for people and for the planet. To show her respect, Sunshine pinned a medal on her little partner, officially making the moon the Admiral. Now whenever someone looks up at the moon, they admire not only its physical beauty but more importantly its inner beauty. Still, old habits are hard to break and once a month the moon goes into hiding and disappears from the sky. On that night we remember that respect comes from inside ourselves even when the moon is not shining."

Invite students to give examples of what respect "looks like." To get younger students started, have Admiral share some ideas such as: "Helping others find their way at night," "Cleaning up the environment," and "Listening to what your parents say." Then list students' ideas on a T-chart such as the one that follows. Next, ask students to describe what respect "sounds like." Admiral can give examples such as, "I'll help you out," "The little things I do make a difference," and "I'm listening." Introduce the third element "feels like" by asking students, "How does respect feel?" Write down students' ideas on the chart and leave it up in the classroom so ideas can be recorded later as they occur. Ask students to write down their personal responses on the How I Feel Form. For younger students, use the eye and ear shapes in place of the words "looks like" and "sounds like." Hold up the heart shape when discussing how respect feels.

Follow-up Activities: Provide each student with a copy of the Respect poster. Ask students to color the poster and put the completed form inside their Character Builder Notebooks. Younger students can also make their own Admiral puppet.

The Behavior of Respect

 Looks Like   **Sounds Like**

Patting someone on the back.	"What a great idea! I never thought about it that way."
Waiting to take a turn.	"I need to be quiet. Mom is sleeping."
Listening without interrupting.	"You shouldn't talk like that about my friend. It isn't nice."
Holding the door open for someone.	"Could you use some help?"
Nodding.	"I'm sorry I offended you."
Winking.	"It's going to all work out!"
High fives.	"Excuse me..."
Thumbs up!	"Pardon me."
Handshake.	"I don't want to infringe on your privacy."
	"Let me open the door for you."
	"Please, may I help you carry the groceries?"
	"Thank you."

GO/STOP RESPECT LANGUAGE   `RS 2`

Purpose: To help students understand the difference between respectful and disrespectful behaviors.

Thought: *If you must choose, take a good name rather than great riches; for to be held in loving esteem is better than silver and gold.*—The Bible

Materials:
- Starter/Stopper Form (RS2d and RS2e).
- Chalk and blackboard, or chart paper and felt pens.
- Character Builder Notebooks (RS1c).

For younger students:
- Respectful Pictures (RS2b) and Disrespectful Pictures (RS2c); one slightly enlarged copy of each and masking tape.
- Stopper and Starter Signs (RS2d and RS2e); one duplicated on red and one on green construction paper; one per student.
- Admiral the Moon Puppet (RS1b).

Note: To adapt this activity for younger or non-writing students, enlarge the forms, Respectful Pictures and Disrespectful Pictures, slightly on a copying machine. Cut out the

RS2d

RS2e

individual pictures and use them for the T-chart activity in place of words. Younger students can also have individual Starter and Stopper puppets by duplicating the forms and attaching them with tape or staples to rulers, paper towel tubes or wooden dowels. Consider using Admiral the Moon Puppet to role play these concepts with students.

Procedure: Begin by creating a T-chart. On the blackboard or on large chart paper write the word "Respect." Make a large "T" shape under the word. On the left of the "T" write the term "Starters/Respectful" and to the right of the "T" write "Stoppers/Disrespectful." Tape the Starter Sign above the "Sounds Like" section and the Stopper Sign above "Doesn't Sound Like." Explain that the green "Sounds Like" column are things that respectful people say. The green "starter" stands for "Go" language, the kinds of things to remember to say because they will help students gain friends and a good reputation, be thought of well by others and earn respect. The "stopper" side of the column on the right is for the kinds of statements people who are not respectful would say. These are statements other people would not think highly of. Tell students: "If you said these kinds of statements, people would not think as highly about you. These are called 'stoppers' because they stop people from gaining respect."

To get younger students thinking about what GO and STOP language sounds like, use the puppet to give examples of what the Admiral Character Builder Puppet would say. For instance, GO statements might include: "I'll help you," "We can clean up the environment," "Listen to your parents," and "I can make a difference." STOP statements might include: "It's no use trying to help anyone," "I'm not as good as the sun," and "I don't know what I can do to help."

Review the term "respect" and ask students to think of times they or someone they were with acted respectfully. You might need to provide a few examples: Sally's grandmother walked into the room and the children stood up to greet her; Bobby opened the door for his mother and waited for her to walk through first; Ruben waited until his teacher was finished talking before sharing his idea; Jim looked at his neighbor's collection of miniature soldiers and didn't touch them, afraid they might break. Remind students that acting respectfully means showing consideration toward themselves, other people and things.

Ask students to think of statements a respectful person might say. Write these ideas under the "starters" section. If students have a difficult time generating comments, go back to the examples given above. What might the grandmother say when the children stand to greet her?

After a few examples, move to the right side and ask students to think of statements someone who was not acting respectfully might say. These are "stopper" statements because they might hurt someone or something. Write these examples on the board.

Leave the chart on the wall so additional comments from students can be added under the "starters" side as they occur in the classroom. Students will begin to focus on respectful actions and statements as the trait is accentuated.

RESPECT

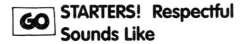 **STARTERS! Respectful Sounds Like**

STOPPERS! Disrespectful Does Not Sound Like

"Excuse me." "Pardon me." "Please go ahead, I can wait." "Please, can I help?" "Thank you for helping." "I'm sorry I offended you." "I know you wouldn't want anyone to read your thoughts without asking." "Wow, you did a great job on your drawing today."	"Hey, I want to talk." "Watch where you're going." "Get to the end of the line. I was here first." "Do it yourself." "Who cares? You should have known better. "So what if I didn't ask first before I read your journal." "Anybody could draw that."

Follow-up Activity: Students can complete their own T-chart for their Character Builder Notebook using the Starter/Stopper Form (RS2d and RS2e). Younger students might draw pictures of respectful and disrespectful behaviors.

Extended Activity: This activity is designed to reinforce the vocabulary of "stoppers" and "starters." With staples or tape, attach the Starter and Stopper Images (RS2d and RS2c) to rulers or paper towel tubes for each student. Admiral the Puppet then calls out a behavior (i.e. "Have a great day," a starter; or "I don't like you," a stopper) and students respond by holding up the correct image.

CALENDAR OF RESPECT RS 3

RS3

Purpose: To reinforce the character builder of respect on a daily basis for a month.

Materials: Calendar of Respect (RS3); one per student.

Thought: *He that will have his son have a respect for him and his orders, must himself have a great reverence for his son.*—John Locke

Procedure: Ask students to put a copy of the Calendar of Respect in their Character Builder Notebook. Explain that for each day of the month students are assigned one activity from the calendar. The activity should be written in their Character Builder Notebook. Students can quickly share the results of their homework assignment with a partner.

RESPECT BOOKLETS

RS 4

Purpose: To help students understand how they can show respect to themselves, others, and property.

Thought: *What you want to be eventually, that you must be every day; and by and by the quality of your deeds will get down into your soul.*—Frank Crane

Materials:
* A blackboard and chalk, or chart paper and marking pens.
* Two 8-1/2 x 11" light-colored pieces of paper, a stapler, crayons or marking pens; per student.

Procedure: Holding pages lengthwise, fold one paper so the finished page is 4-1/4" x 6-1/2". Fold the second page lengthwise so the finished page is 5" x 5-3/4" and place this second page inside the first page. Staple the booklet along the top edge. Help students print these headings along the now indexed booklet:

1. The cover: Ways to Show Respect.
2. The first index: Respecting Self.
3. The second index: Respecting Others.
4. The third index: Respecting Property.

Discuss with students how we can show respect to ourselves, to others and to property. Create three columns on the blackboard or chart paper writing in each column: Self, Others, and Property. Brainstorm with students way to show respect in these three areas and write the ideas generated under the appropriate column. To adapt this activity for younger students, discuss only one area of respect at a time. A few possibilities are provided:

1. *Respecting Self*
   Taking caring of yourself.
   Giving yourself credit.
   Believing you can accomplish anything.
   Eating healthy foods.
   Exercising.
   Talking about yourself kindly.

2. *Respecting Others*
   Being considerate about how others feel.
   Listening with an open mind to other people's ideas.
   Taking turns.
   Not interrupting.
   Treating others the way you want to be treated.
   Respecting other people's privacy.
   Keeping a secret.
   Treating others politely.
   Showing other people courtesy.

3. *Respecting Our Environment/Property*
   Picking up trash.
   Using recycled paper.
   Putting away things you used.
   Treating things carefully.
   Cleaning up after yourself.

Inside the folded index booklet, students work alone or with a partner drawing or writing ways they personally would show respect in each of the three areas.

BILL OF RIGHTS   RS 5

Purpose: To recognize that respect means caring about the rights of others.

Thought: *No man was ever endowed with a right without being at the same time saddled with a responsibility.*—Gerald W. Johnson

Materials:
- Respect Pledge (RS5).
- Blackboard and chalk, or chart paper and marking pens.

Procedure: Explain to students "The Golden Rule" that has guided many civilizations for centuries: "Do unto others as they would do unto you." It means don't treat anybody differently than they would want to be treated themselves. Give each student a copy of the Respect Pledge. Put an enlarged copy of the pledge on a board in a highly visible location so it can be referred to daily. Guide students in practicing the pledge. Each student should sign their pledge form as it is witnessed by another student. The signed Respect Pledge is stored in their Character Builder Notebook.

For older students, you might wish to have a brief discussion about how the Bill of Rights formed the United States of America. Students could each be assigned one of the ten basic rights to study and report to the class. Founding fathers such as Thomas Jefferson, George Washington, Benjamin Franklin, and Alexander Hamilton could also be studied. Older students could also debate their view on which of the ten rights is most important and why.

Ask students to think of the kinds of rights they need to show respect and responsibility in the classroom. You might ask: "How would you like to be treated in this classroom by others?" Students can work in pairs, in quads or as a group to brainstorm a Bill of Rights for themselves. Refer to the rules for brainstorming on Worksheet RT13a of *Responsibility*, the first book in the *Character Builder* series. You might wish to write down all ideas on the blackboard or chart paper for students to vote on their top choices. To speed up this process set a timer to brainstorm only for a certain time frame (i.e. no more than five or ten minutes) and minimize the number of rights to no more than five choices.

When students agree on their Bill of Rights, remind them that the way to show commitment is with the Pledge Shake (see Worksheet RT14 in the *Responsibility* book). Ask students to take a moment to turn to their partners and shake their hand as a sign that they have committed themselves as a class to upholding their newly-developed rights.

Our Bill of Rights

Respect all property.
Respect all people.
Be considerate and raise your hand to share.
Be positive about other people's work.
Be cooperative.
Listen carefully. Don't shout.
Judge people fairly.

Developed by Fourth Graders at Jefferson Elementary in Hays, Kansas.

THE COIN WHIP

Purpose: To gain an awareness of the power of respect and the kinds of behaviors that demonstrate this character builder.

Thoughts: *To receive a present handsomely and in a right spirit, even when you have none to give in return, is to give one in return.*—Leigh Hunt

Literature: *The Table Where Rich People Sit* by Byrd Baylor (Charles Scribner's, 1994). A girl discovers that her impoverished family is rich in things that matter in life, in particular enjoying the outdoors and experiencing nature. This book is a wonderful tool for class-room discussions or journal writing about "What is valuable to you?" and the value of receiving and giving respect. [Third grade and above]

Materials:
- Blackboard and chalk, or chart paper and marking pens.
- A penny (optional).
- *For younger students:* Admiral the Moon Puppet.

Procedure: Gather as a Class Meeting. (Briefly review the Meeting Rules as listed on Worksheet RT8 of *Responsibility*. See chapter 3 for procedure on forming class meetings.) Share with students a discussion facilitator called the Idea Whip. Explain that the Idea Whip is a way we can respectfully hear everyone's ideas and speak in turn. Say: "I'll give you a topic to talk about that everyone knows the answer to. Each person in the circle takes a turn by quickly adding their idea and then passing to the person sitting to their right." Emphasize that the Meeting Rules are still enforced.

To remind students "to whip" ideas quickly and "take turns without interrupting," tell them the talking stick used today will be a penny. Introduce the penny (or Idea Whip) as a "talking chip." The rules are: 1) only the person holding the penny may speak; 2) all eyes and ears should attentively be on the speaker; and, 3) when the speaker is finished, he or she will quickly hand the coin to the person on his or her right. Take a moment to practice the expectation of "handing off" (not throwing) the coin. You may want to use the Admiral Puppet to explain and demonstrate the rules described above.

The "whip topics" on respect are endless. You can choose a different topic each day such as the ones listed below. Write the whip topic on the blackboard or chart paper. Then identify a student as the first speaker and hand him/her the Idea Whip. Students now "whip" the circle, quickly sharing their ideas and passing the chip. Say the topic a few times to remind students and keep them on track. When the circle is completed, students can write their ideas in their Character Builder Notebook.

- "I respect or admire someone who..."
- "A person I respect or admire is _____ because..."
- "One way to show someone you respect them is..."
- "I know someone is not respectful when they..."
- "One way to show an older person respect is..."
- "One way to show a teacher you respect them is..."
- "One way we could show more respect to the earth is..."
- "I look up to people who…"
- "I want to be like someone who…"

For younger students: Admiral the Moon Puppet explains: "One person I really respect and look up to is the sun. No matter what day it is, I can always count on my friend the sun to be there for me and for all the boys and girls on earth. Who is someone you look up to and admire? What about that person do you admire and respect?"

EARNING RESPECT

RS 7

Purpose: To help students recognize respect must be earned.

Thought: *What was least expected is the more highly esteemed.*—Baltasar Gracian

Literature:

- *The Hundred Penny Box* by Sharon Bell Mathis (Puffin, 1975). Michael's love for his great-great aunt, who lives with them, leads him to intercede with his mother who wants to toss out all her old things. What his great aunt collects is a penny for each year of her life. Rich with character themes of respect, loyalty and tradition. [Multicultural: African-American. Third grade and beyond]

- *Three Wishes* by Lucille Clifton (Doubleday, 1992). When a young girl finds a good luck penny and makes three wishes on it, she learns that friendship is her most valued possession. [Primary Age]

Materials: Per student: eight pennies, glue (ideally a hot glue gun), 9 x 36" strip of tagboard (or other heavy paper), stapler, 20" strip of yarn, crayons, marking pens, ruler.

Procedure: Explain that respect means you value and show consideration for someone or something. We show respect by valuing ourselves, each other, and our environment. Ask students to describe ways they can show respect to themselves and others. Ideas such as the ones that follow could be written on the blackboard or on a piece of chart paper.

1. Be considerate towards others.
2. Be a good listener...listen with my eyes and heart.
3. Talk to all kinds of people to find out what they think.
4. Turn off the TV when someone is reading.
5. Don't interrupt Mom.

6. Be polite.
7. Recycle the newspaper.
8. Eat healthy food so I'll be able to do everything I want to do.
9. Congratulate my teammates when they do their best.
10. When I don't agree with my teachers I try to understand their point of view.
11. Leave my friend alone when I know that's what I would want too.
12. Don't say something if it will hurt someone's feelings and it won't help anything.
13. Act true to how I think and feel inside.

Next distribute the tagboard strips and help students mark them into six-inch sections (students could work in pairs.) The strip is then folded accordian-style (first section forward, next section back, next forward and so on). The folds will be crisper and more permanent if creased with a ruler. Staple the yarn piece to the back cover of each booklet for a tie.

Students now make their Earning Respect booklets. Explain that each section represents a different way students can show respect to people or things. In each folded section, ways to earn respect may be drawn or described in words, depending on the students' writing abilities. Using a glue gun, students glue one penny for each section in the booklet as a concrete reminder that respect is earned.

RESPECTFUL VOCABULARY

RS 8

Purpose: To expand students' vocabulary using terminology on the theme of respect.

Respect Vocabulary:
Week 1: Respect
Week 2: Honest
Week 3: Decent
Week 4: Reputable

Thought: *It is astonishing what power words have over man.*—Napoleon Bonaparte

RS8

Materials:
• Bookmark of the Week (RS8); duplicated on light-colored cardstock-weight paper corresponding to the vocabulary word of the week (one per student).
• Chart paper and pens, or blackboard and chalk.

Procedure: Explain that each week you will feature a different vocabulary term that relates to the theme: respect. Give students a copy of the Respect Bookmark. Tell students to study the words on the list. Whenever they learn another word that means almost the same thing as the targeted term, they should add it to their bookmark.

Vocabulary Extensions: Each week a different vocabulary word is written on a large piece of chart paper. New words are added to the list as students develop them. Some teachers use the lists as spelling lists or vocabulary drills. Words can also be used in creative writing and in developing students' knowledge of antonyms. Younger children can draw pictures of the words in their Character Builder Notebook.

School-Wide Adaptations: Many schools feature a "word of the week" which focuses on the monthly theme. Each week one word is printed on a long piece of computer paper and the "banner" is hung on the school walls. A "word of the day" synonymous with the "word of the week" can be announced on the loud speaker.

RESPECTFUL SAYINGS   RS 9

Purpose: To enhance students' awareness of the power of respect.

Thought: *It is well for people who think, to change their minds occasionally in order to keep them clean.*—Luther Burbank

Materials:
- A visible area for hanging sayings (i.e., a bulletin board and push pins, magnets on a file cabinet, a clothes line and clothespins, or a large piece of poster board and glue).
- *For younger students:* Admiral the Moon Puppet.

Procedure: *For younger students:* The Admiral Puppet can introduce the activity by "wearing one of the medals" (attach one of the duplicated paper "medals" to the front of the puppet with double folded masking tape.) Admiral says: "The way I got to be an Admiral was by earning respect from others. I was then presented with medals. Can you tell me ways you could earn respect?" Responses might include: saying nice things to others, using good manners, treating people's things carefully and nicely, treating people the way you'd like to be treated.

Admiral tells students: "Each day I'll be looking for students who are treating themselves, other people or things at this school respectfully. You can help me look for respectful people, too. At the end of the day I'll be giving out medals of respect for respectful children to wear home." Each day Admiral the Moon can announce the names of a few students who acted respectfully, describe what they did or said that was respectful, and award them a medal of respect to proudly wear home.

To begin the activity: Create a board for displaying quotes, comments or sayings about respect. Consider adding a large caption such as, "Give respect in order to get respect." Begin by hanging several positive quotes, newspaper articles, cartoons, sayings or photographs on the board which depict the theme of respect. Encourage students to begin bringing in their own comments and adding them to the board.

Adaptations:
1. Use a quote each day in a "partner sharing" activity. Students read the quotation and discuss its meaning with their partners.

2. A member of the staff or a student committee can read a different quote each day over the loud speaker to set a positive tone.

3. Put a quote about respect on the screen saver of your computer. As soon as students open the computer they will see the quote.

4. Write a different quote regarding respect on the blackboard or chart paper each day. Students copy the quote in their Character Builder Notebooks under a section entitled "Special Sayings."

RESPECTFUL MEDALS   RS 10

Purpose: To reinforce the behavior of respect.

Materials: A few "medals" for students to wear. Medals can be made on a purchased button-maker; or print a design onto cardboard-weight material, then laminate the design for durability. Safety pins can be used to hold the "medal" in place.

Thought: *Some people strengthen the society just by being the kind of people they are.*— John W. Gardner

Procedure: Ask a student committee (or student) to design a button for the theme: Respect. Examples might include a large sun or a saying such as: "I caught you being respectful." The winning button (receiving the most votes from the class) can then be made into medals on a button-making machine.

To begin the activity in the classroom, the teacher wears six medals on the first day. The teacher takes off a medal and pins it onto the first six students who demonstrate respect to another student. The medals then continue to be passed around the classroom/school with one rule: As soon as the "medal wearers" hear another student say a respectful comment or see them perform a respectful deed, they must take off the medal and pin it onto the new respectful sender. Pins continue to roam the classroom until the end of the day when the wearers take off the medals and place them onto a designated bulletin board, where they are stored for the evening.

The next day the last medal wearers take back their medals and continue searching for other respectful students. Medals continue to roam the classroom until a specified time (usually a week or so) when the activity is called to a stop. The activity is a fun way to remind students and staff to be on the alert for respectful behaviors. The medals can then be hung around the room as a reminder of the importance of treating others with respect.

School-Wide Version: At the beginning of the week, provide all staff members with large medals to wear that say: Respect. Be sure to include non-certificated staff in this activity (bus drivers, secretaries, custodians, cafeteria personnel, etc.). When staff members see students displaying "a respectful attitude," they simply take off their medal and pin it onto the deserving students. Awarded students now look for other indivduals on the campus who demonstrate a respectful attitude and the medals continue to be passed around the school/classroom as wearers "catch respectful actions."

Adaptation for Younger Students: Students can create their own medals with a 6" paper plate and 24" length of ribbon. Ask students to draw a way they can earn respect by showing consideration or courtesy to someone. The ribbon length is then overlapped one inch at the top of the paper plate so students can wear the finished medals. This activity helps students recognize different ways to earn respect since they can "see" the depictions on one another's medals. Additional medals can be made to display ways to show respect...to myself...to my teacher...to my parents...to my country...and to property and things

Making The World A Better Place.

To get respect you must earn respect.

_____ is a kid who has our earned respect.

RESPECTFUL THOUGHTS

RS 11

Purpose: To enhance students' awareness of respect through literacy.

Thought: *I like to think of thoughts as living blossoms borne by the human tree.*—James Douglas

Materials:
- A Thought for the Day (RS11a); one per student.
- Respectful Thoughts (RS11b); one per student.

Procedure: There are dozens of possibilities for using the quotations on respect. You may wish to write one Thought for the Day on the board for students to discuss at a Class Meeting or in their Journal. Some teachers have students keep a notebook to record thoughts. Each day students copy the quotation on their worksheets and then write or draw a reflection on what the quotation means to them personally. Daily quotations can also be used within the Study Buddy or Partner Sharing cooperative structures (see chapter 5 in *Responsibility* © Borba).

Bulletin Board: Expand the Thought for the Day activity to a bulletin board. Cut out and post on the board the words: Respectful Thoughts. Then, print a few quotations about respect on colored paper and pin them to the board. Encourage students to be on the look-out for respectful thoughts and deeds and to add them to the board. Consider putting up pictures of some of the more famous authors to accompany their quotes. Finally, ask students to write their own defintions of respect on colored paper and add these to the ones from famous authors.

RESPECT AWARDS

RS 12

Purpose: To reinforce the behavior of respect.

Thought: *Never underestimate the power of simple courtesy. Your courtesy may not be returned or remembered, but discourtesy will.*—Princess Jackson Smith

Materials: Multiple copies of the respect awards run off on bright-colored paper.

Procedure: Stock a stationery-size box with the respect awards and store them in a convenient location. These awards may be presented to students demonstrating respectful behavior or any of the skills taught for this character builder. Each day target a respectful skill and say you'll be looking for students who display the skill. At the end of the class period or school day, take one minute to describe specifically what you saw the student or students doing who displayed the skill that day, then hand them the award. Your praise helps remind students of the exact behavior you are looking for.

The activity can be varied by allowing students to nominate peers who are demonstrating the skill.

BUILDING A CENTER FOR RESPECT

RS 13

Purpose: To increase students' awareness of the importance of respect.

Thought: *Ability will enable a man to get to the top, but it takes character to keep him there.*—Proverb

Materials for the Center:

- Respect Contract (RS13); one per student.
- Bulletin board, cardboard carrel or table top.
- 16 task cards, cut and laminated.
- Shoebox or card stand to store task cards.
- Miscellaneous supplies including glue, scissors, hole punch, stapler, yarn, construction paper scraps, pencils, tape, crayons and marking pens.

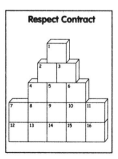

RS13

Materials for the Tasks:

- *Task 2:* colored construction paper scraps, a piece of colored construction paper at least 12 x 18"; large letter templates of the letters in RESPECT; scissors, glue, crayons or marking pens.

- *Task 3:* wire hanger; tagboard templates (at least 6") of the following shapes—circle, triangle, square and diamond.

- *Task 5:* paper tube from a wire clotheshanger; 36" yarn lengths; 12 x 18" piece of construction paper; wallpaper, burlap or fabric.

- *Task 6:* overhead projector; 9 x 12" or 12 x 18" piece of black construction paper; 2-1/2 x 5" white paper strips.

- *Task 7:* a variety of colored construction paper strips 1 x 6"; stapler; dark marking pens.

- *Task 8:* 9 x 12" or 12 x 18" colored construction paper; glue; a pie tin or cookie sheet, and glitter.

- *Task 9:* 9 x 12" colored construction paper; scissors; a colored marking pen; a bulletin board caption that reads, Thumbs UP!

- *Task 10:* Glue, crayons, paper strips cut 3 x 5", paper scraps, yarn. You might wish to designate a certain student each day to be the compliment recipient and rotate this role daily.

- *Task 11:* A cookbook, a few measuring utencils, and a 3 x 5" or 4 x 6" recipe card per student.

- *Task 12:* A ruler; 12 x 18" piece of paper; a large circle shape at least 6" in diameter to trace; a pencil, crayons or marking pens.

Procedure: If you have limited space or do not have a permanent classroom, consider stocking a box with art supplies that can be taken out or brought with you each time you do a Character Builder activity. Set up the Center display in a convenient area of your classroom.

Mount the task cards on heavy paper. Cut them in half and laminate for durability. Store all the materials needed to complete the tasks at the Center (these are indicated on the task cards as well as in the list above). Students may complete the tasks in any order.

Respect Commercial   1

Write a commerical about respect. Try to sell respect so others will want to start using it. For instance, say something positive that might happen in the world if more people showed respect to one another.

Respect Collage   2

1. Cut out large letters from construction paper that spell out the word: RESPECT.

2. Paste the letters on a large piece of poster board.

3. Draw pictures or paste magazine pictures beneath each letter that show different ways you can show respect to others.

Respect Mobile 3

1. Cut out at least 4 shapes from heavy paper. Use the templates to trace around.

2. On the front of each shape, draw or cut out pictures of ways you can show respect to yourself, other people and property.

3. On the back of the shape, write or describe what you would do to be successful in your choice.

4. Tie your shapes to the hanger.

You need: paper, paper punch, magazines, templates.

Rap 4

1. Work alone or with a partner to create a song, a rap, or a chant about respect.

2. Your words should tell why respect is important and how it could make the world a better place.

3. Write the finished rap on a piece of paper.

4. Be ready to present the rap to the group.

Respect Banner 5

1. Make a banner about respect. You could make it from cardboard, burlap, material, wallpaper or construction paper.

2. Decorate your banner with pictures and word cut-outs that show respect. You could include ways to show respect to yourself, other people and property.

3. Staple or tape your finished banner to a paper tube from a wire clotheshanger. Tie on both ends and hang it up.

You could use: paint, paper cut-outs, stitchery, yarn, felt-tipped pens, magazines and crayons.

Respectful Character 6

1. Draw a picture of your head and cut it out. Or make your silhouette by standing in front of an overhead projector. Have a friend trace the silhouette that appears on a piece of paper taped on the wall.

2. Cut out your silhouette.

3. What kinds of things would a respectful character do? Write or draw at least 8 characteristics of respectful people inside the silhouette.

Synonym Chains

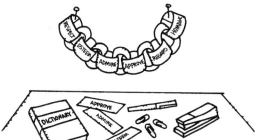

1. Look up the word "respect" in a dictionary.

2. Find at least 10 different words that mean almost the same thing as "respect." These words are called synonyms.

3. Write each synonym on a paper strip.

4. Link your paper strips together to make a chain and staple the ends of each link.

5. Now staple your chain to someone else's chain.

You need: dictionary, pen, stapler, 10 paper strips.

Sparkle Statements

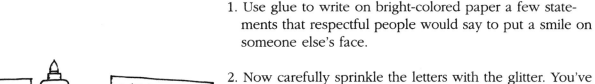

1. Use glue to write on bright-colored paper a few statements that respectful people would say to put a smile on someone else's face.

2. Now carefully sprinkle the letters with the glitter. You've made Sparkle Statements!

3. Sprinkle the remaining glitter into the cookie sheet so it can be used again.

You need: paper, glue, a pie tin or cookie sheet, and glitter.

Put-Ups 9

1. Make a fist with your hand and hold your thumb up. Have a classmate help you trace your hand around a piece of colored paper.

2. Cut it out and make at least four thumbs-up cut-outs.

3. Now print inside each thumbs-up a different respectful put-up statement you could say to someone.

4. Save the thumbs-up to pin up on the THUMBS UP bulletin board.

You need: paper, scissors, and a marking pen.

Compliments 10

1. Use paper to decorate a paper bag making it look like your face. Add your features with crayons, paper scraps or marking pens. Create hair with paper strips or yarn lengths.

2 Now write your classmates respectful compliments and place them in their bags. Make sure to write a compliment to the designated "Kid of the Day."

You need: glue, crayons, paper strips cut 3 x 5", paper scraps, plates, yarn, hole punch.

Respect Recipe 11

Recipe for Respect

Name

Respect Ingredients

Directions

1. Create a recipe for respect. List at least five important ingredients that are needed to make a respectful person.

2. Use the cookbook to help you read how recipes are written. You may want to include terms such as: cup, stir, bowl, mix together, bake, tablespoon, pinch, teaspoon, whip, add. Write your recipe on the recipe card.

Respect Spoke Graph 12

1. Trace the shape of a large circle in the middle of a piece of paper. In the middle of the circle write: "Why We Should Be Respectful."

2. Now use a ruler to draw at least 8 spokes around the circle. Work with a friend to think of at least 8 reasons why being respectful makes the world a better place.

3. Draw or write a different benefit of respect on each spoke.

Bumper Sticker   13

1. Design a bumper sticker about respect.

2. Include on the bumper sticker:
   a. the word "Respect";
   b. a motto or slogan for why you should use it; and,
   c. at least three words that describe it.

You need: marking pens, ruler, 6" x 18" construction paper, scissors.

Respect Story   14

1. To make a movie about respect, cut a long strip of butcher paper 3 x 36" (or use adding machine tape).

2. Roll each of the ends around a pencil and tape the ends to the pencil.

3. Use crayons, colored pencils or ink pens to draw a scene of what respect looks and sounds like in action.

4. Roll up the movie to tell the story to a friend.

Campaign Poster 15

Vote for . . .
RESPECT

It will make the school a warm and secure place to be!

_____
_____
_____
_____

Signed _____

Make a campaign poster about respect. Make sure you include the word "Respect" and two reasons why someone would want to vote for having respect at your school.

You could use: construction paper, felt pens, crayons, paint, magazine cut-outs and templates.

Diorama 16

1. Cut a small peephole in the end of a box with a removable lid.

2. Make a slot in the top of the box to let in light.

3. Cut along three sides of the slot and fold back the flap.

4. Inside the box, make a scene that shows you acting respectfully. Show in the scene how the trait of respect can have a positive impact.

You need: paper, scissors, marking pens, glue and a box with a removable lid.

 3

Creating a Respectful Learning Environment

KEY CONCEPTS:
- Accentuating Respect
- Eliminating Disrespect
- Identifying the Language of Respect/Disrespect

3

Creating a Respectful
Learning Environment

*If you think in positive terms,
you will achieve positive results.*
--NORMAN VINCENT PEALE

A sense of security can exist only in a respectful, positive environment, that is, one in which students immediately perceive they are welcomed and appreciated. Students will bond to such an atmosphere. They will feel that it is their classroom; it is where they are cared for and where they belong. Such feelings are obviously conducive to learning because students are more willing to participate, attend and behave appropriately. Our students' attitudes toward learning cannot be separated from the educational climate; it is the combination of these two factors that create a powerful force for learning.

CHARACTER BUILDER STEP #2

Create a Respectful Learning Environment

Helping students maintain respectful attiutudes is no easy task, particularly when we must deal with students who are negative. One reason these individuals are so difficult is that no matter how positive we are, their negative attitude ("I don't want to," "I'm dumb!", "I can't do this") continues to perpetuate itself. Negativism has a domino effect: it spreads wherever negative statements are made. By the same token positive, respectful statements are contagious. Therefore, it is easier to maintain a positive environment when posiitve models are available.

For this reason, negative statements are particularly detrimental to a learning climate. Disrespectful statements tend to create larger and more hurtful messages. Ridicule, put-downs and name-calling can escalate far too quickly, breaking down emotional safety and replacing it with an environment of fear, tension and dread. There's another reason why educators need to quickly squelch student negativism, disrespect and put-downs: there is an inescapable correlation between these acts and more serious student violence.

"Research has shown a direct connection between serious acts of violence and the more subtle forms of 'harm' such as pushing, shoving, name-calling and various other forms of harrassment and neglect. Educators and other school personnel can do a lot about 'nipping in the bud' these more subtle forms of harm before they grow into seriously violent acts." (Student Aggression by A.P. Goldstein, B. Harootunian, & J.C. Conoley, New York: Guilford, 1994).

Growing numbers of educators recognize how impossible it is to have a healthy learning environment if the school and classrooms are not emotionally safe. Dramatic changes can happen when the school staff deliberately "tunes up" and "turns on" the traits of positivism by teaching students the skills of acquiring a positive attitude and then reinforcing appropriate positive behaviors. Not only will students be better prepared to deal constructively with difficulties, but the learning environment can become a haven of emotional safety that so many of our students crave.

Steps to a Respectful Atmosphere

To Build Respect
1. Model respectful statements.
2. Accentuate respect.
3. Build awareness of positive, respectful language.
4. Label appropriate respectful language.
5. Reinforce respectful statements.
6. Practice respectful atittude skills.
7. Teach how to receive compliments.

To Eliminate Disrespect
1. Draw awareness to negativity and disrespect.
2. Label disrespect.
3. Teach skills to defuse disrespect.
4. Teach skills to replace negativity.

Steps to Accentuate Respect

Many of today's students lack an understanding of respect because their experiences with this character builder trait have been minimal. Think about it: If you are rarely around people who display respect and if you aren't treated as though you are a valued and worthwhile individual, how can you possibly "catch the behavior?" That's the secret of learning character building behaviors—they're caught by watching others do them well. Today's schools and classrooms are enormously significant institutions because for many students these places may be the only times appropriate character building traits can be taught. If you recognize this premise, you'll also recognize the power of educators. Tune up the behavior you want to be caught and accentuate it. Here's how!

1. Model respectful statements. Never forget how you impact your students—you may very well be their only model of respect! You may wish to say respectful statements so that the class may hear you: "Thank you, Mrs. Smith, for sharing your slides with us. We really appreciated them." Or, "Excuse me, Sally, I didn't mean to interrupt you." For many students this may be the only time they hear what respect sounds like.

2. Accentuate respect. In any environment, establish a firm commandment, "You may not talk hurtfully about yourself or others." Put it in your own words if you like, but post it in a highly visible location, such as on the door, along the length of the chalkboard, or on a bulletin board.

3. Build awareness of respectful language. Like it or not, we have become a negative, disrespectful society that too often emphasizes sarcasm, put-downs and disrespect. Listen to the popular sit-coms on television and count the frequency of statements based on negativity, ridicule and sarcasm. Studies show the average student is watching a minimum of three hours of television a night. Many of today's students are reared in homes seeping in disrespect and negativity. The character builder skills of respect are foreign to many of our students. Some students do not know what respectful language is and need to be taught the skill. As a group, students can brainstorm statements that show respect and post them as a reminder that there are other choices to replace disrespect.

4. Label appropriate positive language. Many students need help in distinguishing between appropriate language and destructive language. They may have said disrespectful put-down statements so often they've conditioned themselves to say the negative. It is helpful to label appropriate and inapproprpiate language for the students. Terms that can be used to describe appropriate respectful language include "fuzzy," "compliment," builder-upper," "booster," "sparkler," and "validator." Inappropriate disrespectful language can be labeled by terms such as "disrespectful," "zinger," "terminator," "put-down," "prickly," "detonator," or "killer." Choose one term from each category, teach it to students and then consistently use it to label character building language. For example, say, "That's a put-up," or "That's a put-down." Remember, your attempts at teaching students the skills of positive, respectful language will be greatly enhanced if students hear the same key phrases, encouragement, vocabulary and tone.

5. Reinforce respectful statements. Reinforce what you want to be repeated. Try to key in on the students' respectful statements and forget the disrespectful ones for awhile. It's easier to change behavior by focusing on the positive aspects instead of the negative. Some students, however, make that very tough to do and will almost provoke you to put them down. If you remember that you're only hooking into their game if you do, it'll be easier to stay focused on the respectful.

Every once in awhile try reinforcing respectful statements and actions with more than verbal recognition. A pat on the back, a phone call home and a message gram are just a few ways to acknowledge deserving students. Use the respectful message grams provided in this manual (See RS14c). Make ample copies and stock an activity center with the message grams. Students can then be encouraged to give them out to one another. Remember, peers can be a powerful force in making respectful atittudes an epidemic in your environment.

6. Practice respectful behavior skills. Listing respectful statements on a poster, while helpful, is not enough to change students' behavior. Students must be given opportunities to practice respectful behavior. In many cases, positive character building skills will be unfamiliar to your students; they may not have been exposed to the skills frequently enough for mastery or they may never have been exposed to them at all. We can no longer assume today's students have acquired any of the skills.

Keep in mind that many students may not be comfortable saying respectful statements. These students should be allowed to choose the kinds of statements that they feel safe saying. "Hello," "Hi," "How are you?" or a smile and eye contact are appropriate first steps for these students. Forcing someone to say respectful statements makes them insincere.

Steps to Eliminate Disrespect

We all know changing habits takes time and effort. Many students have been locked into saying and displaying disrespectful words and behaviors for years. We certainly can't expect overnight success. Expect skill backsliding for awhile in which a child will start to demonstrate the new skill, then when you think they have moved up a notch on the respect ladder, the next day they're back to where they had been or worse off than they were before. These are normal patterns since our behavior tends to resort to what we're most comfortable with—that's why habits are so difficult to change. Don't despair and never give up! You can help children learn more respectful behaviors by slowly replacing their old disrespectful habits. These techniques show you ways to replace the older habits with newer, more appropriate ones. The most important rule for your success is: be consistent.

1. Draw awareness to disrespect. When students go against the "respect commandment," be careful not to be negative toward their already disrespectful disposition. Disrespect quickly breeds disrepect. Casually mention, "Remember, we only say respectful words." Some teachers use a private code or signal between themselves and their students. Each time students make a disrespectful comment, the teacher says a word like "Zap!" or uses a signal (such as raising a hand) as a reminder to stop.

"He has the right to criticize who has the heart to help."
—Abraham Lincoln

Often students are not aware of how many disrespectful statements they are saying. One way to bring them to this awareness is to use a simple tally system. On paper, designate one column for respectful statements, the other for disrespectful ones. Each time students make either a respectful or disrespectful comment, they add a stamp or mark to the appropriate side.

Another way to help students become aware of disrespectful statements is to use tokens (i.e., marbles, poker chips, peanuts). Students hold tokens in the left pocket, and whenever they make a disrespectful statement, a token is transferred to the right pocket. Often just one reminder will get the message across.

2. Label disrespect…Call it! Students need to recognize disrespectful put-downs by saying a code word or making a sound immediately back to the sender. The code should be agreed upon by all students so that they recognize it. Words such as "disrespectful put-down," "pricklie," "killer," "zinger" or sounds such as "ouch," "buz-z-z" or "ding-a-ling" will make the sender aware that the statement was inapropriate.

3. Teach skills to defuse disrespect. If the objective is to squelch disrespect on campus, then it is critical to teach everyone (peers and staff) to take the same steps in handling disrespectful actions. "Defuser" skills can calm disrespectful behaviors before they detonate into a full explosion (usually physical or verbal retaliation). Make it a campus rule that disrespectful statements are not allowed. Whenever a put-down is said, teach the rule that the sender must then change the put-down into a "put-up." *The rule is: One Put-Down = One Put-Up or One Disrespectful Statement = One Respectful Statement.* In some schools this rule is even more stringent: for every put-down there must be three put-ups. Whatever the number, the rule must be consistently enforced to be effective.

4. Teach skills to replace negativity. Many of our students are locked into disrespectful, inappropriate behavior patterns simply because they don't know what to do instead. Asking them to "Be more respectful" or "Act nicer" has no value if the student does not know how to demonstrate the skills of respect or kindness. These skills need to be taught. The activities in this chapter teach students to replace disrespectful behaviors with respectful behaviors. Keep in mind, however, that new behaviors take a tremendous amount of repetition and commitment before they can replace the older, more comfortable habits. Students will slip back easily into older disrespectful behavior patterns unless the newer skills of respect are continually reinforced and practiced. Consistency and reinforcement are critical. Don't give up, though! Respectful attitudes are contagious.

Activities to Enhance Student Respect

The activities listed below are taken from the *Esteem Builders* series written by Dr. Michele Borba.

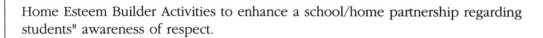

Code	Activity	Page

Esteem Builder Activities to help students develop positive attitudes and respectful language.

S25	Smile Book	63
S26	Super Sparkle Gram	63
S28	Smile File	64
S29	Smile Cans	64
S30	Builder-Uppers	65

School-Wide Activities (from *Esteem Builders*).

SW3	Positive Performers	387
SW4	Positive Performance Award	381
SW29	Positive Comments Contest	381

Concept Circles (from *Esteem Builders*).

CC1	Beginning Circle	326
CC25	Sunshine Statements	335
CC26	Sparkle Box	336
CC32	Silent Sparkles	338
CC33	Word Gifts	338
CC34	Word Power	338
CC40	Compliments	340
CC41	Compliment Hanging	340
CC35	Glasses Circles	339

Home Esteem Builder Activities to enhance a school/home partnership regarding students" awareness of respect.

HEB2	Positive Reinforcement	197
HEB5	Changing Negative Messages	200

Home Esteem Builder Grams to send to parents regarding respect and positive attitudes.

Gram #4	Increasing Positivism	149

Staff resources in *Staff Esteem Builders*.

SEB37	Balloon Pop	66
SEB39	Terrific Teacher Notes	66

Respectful Language

Purpose: To teach students the language of respect or "builder-uppers."

Thought: *Speak ill of no man, but speak all the good you know of everybody.*--Proverb

Materials:
- Respectful Openers (RS14a); one per student.
- Respectful Messages (RS14c); one duplicated poster size.
- Marking pens, crayons or colored pencils.
- Chart paper and marking pens, or blackboard and chalk.
- For younger students: 2 pieces of 12 x 18" light-colored construction paper.

Divide students into pairs. Provide each pair with a Respectful Openers form. Tell students their task is to create a list of respectful "builder-upper comments." These are respectful comments that a student could say to another student that would put a smile on his/her face. Tell students that the words we say to one another can be either respect makers or breakers. Instruct the teams to take 10 minutes to come up with words, phrases or sentences that would put a smile on another student's face. Each team must then design their own Respectful Openers poster using the form.

At the end of 10 minutes, each team shares their poster, and a few words of their choice with the rest of the class. The teacher can print some of these ideas on poster-size chart paper to visibly hang in the classroom as a reminder. Laminate completed posters and use as a bulletin board display.

Refer to the Brainstorming Rules poster (see *Responsibility* RT13a) to remind students of the rules: every idea counts, no put-downs are allowed, and students are free to piggy back or add on to the ideas of others. Set a time limit of no more than five minutes to brainstorm respectful, builder-upper comments. Write all ideas down on the chart paper or blackboard. Leave the chart hanging and now provide students with a copy of Respectful Openers. Working ideally with a partner, students create their own list of Respectful Openers on the form. The finished form is stored in their Character Builder Notebooks. Share with students the skill builder Respectful Messages. (RS14c)

Adaptation for Younger Students: Provide each student with two pieces of light-colored construction paper (12 x 18"). Tell students to rule off a door shape 3" from the top and sides. Using a ruler, draw a straight 15" line from the bottom of the "door" to the bottom edge of the paper. Cut along the 15" vertical line, stopping 3" from the top. Now cut a 6" horizontal line, stopping 3" from the left side of the page.

Carefully fold the opened "door," creasing it from the top 3" to the bottom. Glue this cut piece to the same size section on the paper, keeping the folded door section unglued. Ask students to decorate the outside of their door with a doorknob and the word "Door Openers." On the inside of the door and on the second piece of paper students can print door opening words of courtesy and consideration for others. Hang the finished doors on a bulletin board display.

Follow-up Activities: Students can work in groups to create a project about respect. Choose any of the ideas from Respect Projects (RS14b) and ask students to show what the trait means and why it's important.

The Keys of Courtesy   RS 15

Purpose: To learn the respectful language of courtesy and manners.

Thought: *Manners are the happy way of doing things.*—Ralph Waldo Emerson

Literature: *My Dog Never Says Please* by Suzanne Williams (Dial, 1997). Ginny Mae Perkins has atrocious manners and her family keeps reminding her. She cannot eat face down in her plate; she has to wear shoes; she must clean up her room. The book tells a fanciful story with a poet's sense of words and a great moral.

Materials:
• Keys of Respect (RS15); duplicate one per student on bright-colored construction.
• Paper, scissors, marking pens.
• Blackboard and chalk, or chart paper and marking pens.

For younger students:
• Admiral Puppet (RS1b).
• Eye and Ear Images (RS1f and RS1g); duplicated and cut out; masking tape for hanging.

Procedure: Provide students with a copy of the Keys of Respect and ask them to cut out the key along the outside margin. For younger students use the Admiral Puppet to hand out the keys as he tells students he is giving them keys to the universe that will open doors for them now and in the future. Then have the puppet teach students the refrain:

   Respect like doors will open with ease, if you learn to use these keys.

Explain that one of the easiest ways to show respect and at the same time enhance your reputation is by using good manners and acting politely. Take a moment to brainstorm with students a list of good manner keys. For older students, create the list on a T-chart for courtesy. For younger students, attach the ear image to the "Sounds Like" side of the chart and the eye image to the "Looks Like" side with masking tape as shown below.

COURTESY

Sounds Like	Looks Like
please	waiting patiently
thank you	taking turns
excuse me	using appropriate language
pardon me	covering your mouth when you cough
I'm sorry	not interrupting
Can you forgive me?	

Now assign each student a partner and give each team the RS15 Respectful Keys Form. Students are to write on their key a statement or behavior of courtesy that they could use to show respect. Students then take turns practicing the phrases with one another. The finished keys can be pinned onto a bulletin board with the caption: "Keys of Respect."

Labeling Respect/Disrespect   RS 16

Purpose: To create a common language school/class-wide for calling respectful language "put-up" statements and disrespectful language "put-down" statements.

Thought: *I will not judge my brother until I have walked two weeks in his moccasins.*— Sioux Indians

Materials:
• Starter/Stopper Form (RS2a).
• Chart paper and colored markers, or blackboard and chalk.

For younger students:
• Starter and Stopper Signs (RS2d and RS2e); one of each duplicated on red and green con struction paper respectively and cut out.

Procedure: Call students to a Class Meeting and briefly review the Meeting Rules. Inform students there are many different ways to label words that are respectful and disrespectful. Remind students that respectful messages are put-up statements that show consideration for others and let people know you value them. Disrespectful statements are put-downs that show no consideration for others. When you say these statements people think less of you. Emphasize, "What's important is for everyone to be in agreement with the words and to use the same words." Note: This activity can also be conducted over the loud speaker for a school-wide vote.

Draw a T-chart on the blackboard or chart paper writing "Put-Downs: Disrespectful" on the left of the T and "Put-Ups: Respectful" on the right side. For younger students, tape the red circle or Stopper Sign on the left and the green circle or Starter Sign on the right. Explain that in the next few minutes the class will brainstorm possible terms for put-ups and put-downs. Briefly review the rules for brainstorming (see *Responsibility* RT13a) and then for three minutes list the possibilities. Ask the class to vote for which terms they wish to use and circle the top choice for both categories.

 **Put-Downs** **Put-Ups**

Put-Downs	Put-Ups
Disrespectful	Respectful
Detonators	Uplifters
Exterminators	Sparkles
Killers	Builder-uppers
Zingers	Sparklers
Pokes	Strokes
Negatives	Positives
Slugs	Sunshine
Pricklies	Fuzzies
	Compliments
	Boosters
	Validators

Model to students how to "call it" when a person slips up and says a disrespectful "stopper" message, for example, say: "That's a put-down."

Follow-up Activity: Students can make their own T-chart of disrespectful and respectful vocabulary for their Character Builder Notebooks using the Starter/Stopper Form (RS2a).

RS 17

Extinguish Disrespect

Purpose:
• To create an emotionally safe and respectful learning environment.

- To teach students a common signal to defuse disrespectful actions and words.
- To set an expectation of how to treat others in the classroom: "No Disrespect is Allowed" and "Treat Others with Consideration."

Thought: *The moon could not go on shining if it paid any attention to the little dogs that bark at it.*—Anonymous

Materials:
For younger students:
- Eye and Ear Images (RS1f and RS1g); duplicated and cut out.
- Stopper and Starter Signs (RS2d and RS2e); one of each duplicated on red and green construction paper respectively and cut out.
- Masking tape for hanging.
- Admiral Puppet (RS1b).

Procedure: Draw a "Looks Like/Sounds Like" T-chart on the blackboard or chart paper with the word "Respect" at the top. Begin by explaining the expectation: "Disrespect is not allowed." Also explain the purpose of the expectation, saying, "In this school we want to make sure everyone feels included and safe about being here. You can make people feel that way by the kinds of words you say." Ask students to think of words that "build you up inside."

Then list these on or add them to a "Looks Like/Sounds Like" chart. Respectful words that help students succeed and make them feel included might be: "Great!" "Thank you!" "Can I help you?" "What do you need?" "It was fun working with you."

List "put-ups" for respectful, positive, builder-upper behavior and "put-downs" for disrespectful, sarcastic, judgmental, negative behavior on two separate charts.

RESPECT
Put-Ups

 Looks Like

Sounds Like

Looks Like	Sounds Like
A smiling face.	"Way to go!"
A nodding head.	"Can I help?"
Pat on friend's back.	"What can I do?"
A high five.	"Thanks for the help."
A handshake.	"I'm glad you're here."
Grin.	"You can do it!"
Wink.	Saying something positive.
Touch on the arm.	Paying attention.
	Saying words that build someone up.
	Not being critical.
	Listening without interrupting.

DISRESPECT
Put-Downs

 Looks Like

Sounds Like

Looks Like	Sounds Like
Rolling eyes.	"You're stupid!"
Laughing at person.	"That's dumb!"
Eyes looking down.	"Shut up!"
Making a face.	"You look weird."
Snarling the nose.	"Go somewhere else."
Pointing with finger.	Using sarcastic tone.

Follow-up activity for younger students: Tape or staple the Stopper and Starter traffic signals to a ruler, paper towel tube or wooden dowel and role play respectful and disrespectful words with students. Using the Stopper and Starter lists and the Admiral Puppet, call out an item randomly and ask, "Stopper or starter?" Students can either verbally respond with "stopper" or "starter," or they can hold up either a small red construction paper circle (for stopper) or green paper circle (for starter). If Admiral, for instance, says, "Thanks for the help," students would call out "starter" (or hold up a green circle). "Rolling eyes" would have students respond with "stopper" or a red circle. Play the game for five minutes or so to review the terms respectful and disrespectful.

What Disrespect Feels Like   RS 18

Purpose: To help students understand the effect of disrespectful statements.

Thought: *He has a right to criticize who has a heart to help.*—Abraham Lincoln

Materials:
- Heart Image (RS1h); duplicated on red or pink construction paper (the larger the better, especially if doing the activity at a school-wide assembly). Print the word "respect" in the middle of the heart with a thick black marking pen.
- Admiral Puppet (RS1b).
- Burner Puppet (RS18).

Procedure: Begin the activity by saying, "We want everyone to feel good and safe about being at school and that's why we have an expectation to say only respectful, builder-upper statements...statements that build other people up. I expect you to say only the kinds of statements you'd want someone to say to you. Sometimes it's not what you say but what your body does that sends a respectful message to another person. Show me the kinds of things you could do with your body that show respect." Responses might include: smiling, winking, nodding, giving a high five, making eye contact.

Now describe the effect of being disrespectful or putting others down. Say, "Every time someone says a disrespectful message it tears a bit of their feelings away." Demonstrate by tearing a piece of the construction paper heart. Say, "We've probably all had the experience of having someone tell or give us put-downs." Ask students to give a few examples of words or statements that are disrespectful put-downs. "You're stupid," "What an idiot," "You're dumb." With each example tear off another part of the heart.

Tell students that not only words but the tone of voice, such as saying a respectful message sarcastically, and even posture and facial expressions, such as grimacing, raised eyebrows, and frowns, can be interpreted as disrespectful put-downs. Role play a few examples with students and again tear off another piece of the heart signifying how disrespect destroys feelings.

Admiral and the Torn Heart

For younger students, use the puppet to tell the story of Admiral and the Torn Heart. Say, "Admiral earned the respect not only of the sun and the many people he had helped, but of the millions of stars throughout the universe as well. His reputation spread beyond this galaxy into other galaxies where it was said he could do things the bigger and brighter sun could not. He soon earned a position on the universal police force where his valuable advice on nighttime law and order reformed the organization and promoted peace between the galaxies.

"Unfortunately, when Admiral took on his new position, this meant Burner the Meteor was no longer Chief of Nighttime Patrol. On learning he had lost his position to the moon, the meteor became filled with rage and jealousy, swelling to three times its normal size and fueling a heat that melted a nearby asteroid within its stormy interior. Watching as Admiral received signs of respect and congratulations at an installation dinner, Burner vowed he would get even if it was the last thing he did in his lifetime. If he could make Admiral feel bad about himself, Burner thought, the moon would give up his job and go back to being a little nobody in the sky.

"Burner's first choice of attack was to destroy Admiral's self-respect or how he felt about himself. He knew the moon took pride in its beautiful smooth, shiny face, so the next morning the meteor streaked across a couple of galaxies and came screeching to a stop within a few miles of the moon. Looking up into the face of the moon, Burner said, 'You're ugly.' The moon tried to ignore the comment, but he couldn't ignore the pain he felt in his heart. (Tear a piece of the construction paper heart.) The smile on Admiral's face drooped a little and, with Burner's hot breath too close for comfort, the medals that had been pinned on his chest during the installation dinner began to rattle from fear. 'You're ugly, and I'm going to prove it to you,' Burner said again, grimacing. (Tear a piece of the construction paper heart.)

"The meteor thundered and circled madly in the moonlit night sky as it picked up top speed. Then Burner bolted in a straight line towards Admiral, sinking the weight of his burning body in the face of the moon. That's when the meteor noticed that the hole he had made on the face of the moon was just one of hundreds of holes called craters. From a distance the surface of the moon had looked perfectly smooth, but the truth was lots of meteors had accidentally landed on Admiral over the centuries. 'So, you're not so beautiful after all,' Burner laughed when he discovered Admiral's secret. 'I'm going to tell everybody what I saw and we'll see what they think of you then.' (Tear a piece of the construction paper heart.) Admiral felt wounded but there was nothing he could do to stop Burner from spreading his tale.

"The first place Burner went with his story was the sun. 'Guess what I found out. The moon isn't beautiful like you thought he was. He has a face full of craters.' Sunshine smiled and said, 'Why Burner, I already know that. That's why I gave him a beautiful light for clothing.' Burner could see he was getting no where with the sun, so he sped off to his own galaxy where he found a planet named Petunia and told her the same thing he had told the sun. "Oh, well, I have some pretty big canyons in me too,' she said. 'But I heard he's covered in moonlight. Wouldn't that be a beautiful thing to have?' Burner didn't answer her. "Idiot!" he thought. Then he rode off in a huff until he came across a star named Sparky. Sparky was a friendly fellow and Burner was sure he'd see his side of the story.

"When Burner told him what he'd discovered on the moon, Sparky responded with amazement. 'The moon has such a beautiful light, why it doesn't even matter what his face looks like. If only all of us could shine as bright.' Burner was losing heat and light as the fury trapped inside his belly began to burn itself out. Noticing the meteor looking a little pale, Sparky asked if he needed any help. Burner said no, that he just needed a good night's sleep. Then the meteor hurried home and fell asleep exhausted. Meanwhile, the positive, respectful words of the sun, star and planet traveled along the lightwaves and healed Admiral's torn heart."

Follow-up Activity: Provide each student with a red construction paper heart measuring 12 x 18" or 9 x 12". Ask students to print in large letters the word "respect" inside the heart. Finally, have students draw or write ways they can show respect to others so their feelings and heart will be pumped up and not torn apart. Finished hearts can be hung on a bulletin board under the caption, "Changing the World One Heart at a Time."

Disrespect Burial

RS 19

Purpose: To help students recognize disrespectful statements are hurtful and not to be tolerated.

Thought: *If it is very painful for you to criticize your friends, you are safe in doing it. But if you take the slightest pleasure in it, that is the time to hold your tongue.*—Alice Miller

Materials:
- 3 x 5" cards; one per student.
- Shoebox size box.
- Shovel.
- *For younger students:* Burner Puppet (RS18) from previous activity.

Procedure: Tell students one way to "get rid of disrespectful put-downs once and for all" is to bury them. Ask students to write the disrespectful put-down statements from the brainstorming session on 3 x 5" cards. Place all the cards into a shoebox size box. The class then buries the box full of put-downs somewhere near the school site.

For younger students: Give examples of disrespectful statements Burner would say, including: "You're ugly," "I don't need your help," and "Idiot!" Write these on the cards along with the ideas generated by students from the brainstorming session. Have them bury the Burner Puppet in the box along with the cards. Tell them the meteor burned itself out and never woke up from his sleep. Hold a funeral for the puppet and ask a student to give a brief "good riddance" eulogy.

Questions for Follow-up Discussion:
- What is a put-down or disrespectful message?
- Tell about a time you were put down and someone was disrespectful to you. How did you feel?
- Where do kids learn to be disrespectful?
- Why do people put themselves down?
- Are there alternatives to disrespect?
- Why is it hard to change to other alternatives?
- How would you feel about being in a "disrespectful free" environment where no put-downs and disrespect are allowed?

Disrespect Signal RS 20

RS 20

Purpose: To reinforce the premise of respect: "Put-downs and disrespectful messages are not allowed." To help students squelch negative, put-down statements that derail a respectful learning climate.

Thought: *When a man points a finger at someone else, he should remember that three of his fingers are pointing at himself.*—Anonymous

Materials: Extinguish Disrespect (RS20); enlarged to poster size.

Procedure: Tell students one of the best ways to stop put-downs is to send back a signal that reminds the sender, "Put-downs are not allowed here." Show students the Extinguish Disrespect poster and point out the upside down thumb signal. Explain that the thumb is not a Thumbs Up sign telling the sender "Good job!" It's a Thumbs Down sign which means, "That was a disrespectful put-down and it's not allowed." Emphasize to students that they are not to say anything to a student who sends them a put-down— just send them the signal. Say, "If everyone remembers to use the signal, we may be able to get rid of put-downs once and for all."

Extended Activity: Provide paper and marking pens for students and ask them to design their own Extinguish Disrespect Posters. If you're using Study Buddy teams (see *Responsibility* chapter 5), each pair can create their own posters. Younger students can decorate their posters with a border of their thumb prints created from an ink pad.

Stamp Out Put-Downs RS 21

Purpose: To remind students that disrespect and put-downs are not allowed.

Thought: *There is little room left for wisdom when one is full of judgment.*—Malcom Hein

Materials:
• Scissors, pencils, colored marking pens.
• Colored construction paper (8-1/2 x11" for younger students; 9 x 12" or larger for older students); the paper must fit the length of the student's foot.

Procedure: Assign students to work with partners and provide each team a pair of scissors, marking pen, and two pieces of colored construction paper. Tell students to quickly take turns tracing around their partner's shoe, then have them cut out the outline. Next remind students that the best way to create a respectful learning atmosphere is to "stamp out disrespect." Briefly review how disrespect can be sent by words, tone of voice, posture, and facial expressions.

Ask students to write or draw on their paper shoe one disrespectful behavior they've received or seen. Now tell students to "stamp it out forever" by turning the shoe over and on the other side writing a "respectful replacer." What respectful word, tone of voice, posture, or facial expression could stamp out disrespect? Place the footprints around the room with the "respectful" side face up and a large caption that reads: "Stamp Out Disrespect."

 4

Showing Respect Towards Others

KEY OBJECTIVES:

- Sending a respectful compliment.
- Developing the skill of encouragement.
- Learning to say an "I like message."

4

Showing Respect
Towards Others

*Man finds his fulfillment and happiness
only in relatedness to and solidarity
with his fellow men.*

--ERIC FROMM

The first two steps to enhance respect are to teach students what this character builder is and to set firm expectations of appropriate behavior. One of the most important expectations is to think before acting: "Is this the way I'd like to be treated by others?" Once the expectations of respect are in place, and your students clearly understand what respect looks and sounds like, you're ready to implement the third step to developing respect: showing students' respect towards others.

CHARACTER BUILDER STEP #3

Showing Respect Towards Others

The third step to developing this character builder, showing respect towards others, is thought by many teachers to be natural: "Shouldn't children just behave respectfully towards others? Why do we have to teach this?" Keep in mind that respectful behavior is far from normal, everyday treatment to many students. There are many skills that, unless they are seen and practiced, may never become part of these children's behavior. Courtesy, manners, showing consideration, and giving someone a compliment —all of these are learned behaviors. This chapter focuses on the behaviors of civility and consideration towards others. By helping children recognize and practice these behaviors, educators enhance students' respectful treatment towards others, which hopefully will extend far beyond the confines of the classroom walls and into society, both now and in the future.

Activities to Enhance Student Respect Towards Others

The activities listed below are taken from the *Esteem Builders* series written by Dr. Michele Borba.

Code	Activity	Page

Esteem Builder Activities to help students develop respect and positive attitudes towards others.

Sending Compliments   RS 22

Purpose: To teach students the skill of complimenting or praising. To help them recognize that disrespect can be shown not only in words but in how the words are said (i.e., tone of voice, posture, body movements, and facial expressions).

Thoughts: *Anything scarce is valuable: praise for example.*—Anonymous

Silent gratitude isn't very much use to anyone.—Anonymous

Most of us can live peacefully with our own faults, but the faults of others get on our nerves.—Anonymous

Materials:
• Sending Compliments (RS22); one per student and one enlarged poster size.

For younger students:
• Eye/Ear/Heart Images (RS1f, RS1g, and RS1h); duplicated and cut out.
• Masking tape for hanging.
• Admiral Puppet (RS1b).

Procedure: At a Class Meeting discuss ways you can share the following: caring thoughts…kind feelings with another person…ways to make the classroom more peaceable.

Write at the top of a T-chart the word: "Compliment." Ask students, "What does it mean to give a compliment to someone?" Give the definition of compliment as "praising or saying something nice about someone." On the left side of the T-chart write "Sounds Like." For younger students, tape the ear image to the chart. Ask students, "What are some ways we can compliment each other?"

Explain to students that words of respect can be turned into disrespect by how they are said. Tone of voice, posture, and facial expressions all can turn respect into disrespect. If words are said in a sarcastic tone, even a respectful, put-up word can become disrespectful. Role play a few examples with students, saying the following words sarcastically: "Way to go," "Wow, did you do a great job," "Nice hair cut." Tone of voice is one way to turn respect into disrespect.

Now refer to the "Looks Like" section of the chart. The eye image can be taped to the chart for younger students. Point out that posture is another way we turn a respectful message into a disrespectful message. Ask students if they can name a few ways to stand that can be disrespectful. Responses include: turning away from the person, walking away when the other person is talking, shrugging shoulders, looking down. Explain that these behaviors are "stoppers"—they stop others from feeling as though we respect or value them.

Describe how facial expressions can send either respectful or disrespectful messages. Role play behaviors such as eye contact on the ground, rolling eyes, grimacing, raised eyebrows all as possible ways disrepect can be sent. Tell students that just as they created a put-down signal to signify disrespectful or put-down words, they should also signal to someone when disrespect is being sent through posture, tone of voice, or facial expressions.

Finally, ask students what "starters" for sending a compliment would look like. Ask, "What are some ways to let someone know we respect them just by looking at us?" These behaviors can be added to the "Looks Like" section on the chart.

Provide students with a copy of "Sending Compliments" and ask them to work in pairs to role play sending positive messages using a respectful tone of voice and facial expressions.

COMPLIMENTS (Starters)

Looks Like

Sounds Like

Looks Like	Sounds Like
Smiling.	"I like your haircut."
Nodding.	"Your drawing looks great!"
Looking eye to eye.	"Cool hat."
No rolling eyes.	"Nice job on your report."
Facing the person.	"Super run."
Standing still.	"I like your outfit."
Head held high.	"Great backpack. Where'd you get it?"
Standing straight.	"Way to go on your paper."
	A sincere voice.
	An upbeat tone.

Extended Activity for Younger Students: On the far right side of the T-chart write "Feels Like." Have the Admiral Puppet ask students, "How does it make you feel when you receive praise/compliment from someone?" Add students' ideas onto the chart.

COMPLIMENTS (Starters)

Happy
Excited
Warm
Positive
Confident
Liked
Approved
Encouraged
Motivated
Pleased
Content
Glad
Satisfied
Affirmed

Compliment Book

RS 23

Purpose: To provide the opportunity for students to compliment and recognize one another.

Thought: *The sweetest of all sounds is praise.*—Xenophon

Literature: *The Best Worst School Year Ever* by Barbara Robinson (Harper Collins, 1994). The six horrible Herdmans, the worst kids in the history of the world, are causing all kinds of mayhem throughout the school year. One classroom assignment is for students to hand in a "compliment paper" describing the special attributes of another student. This book is the perfect read-aloud accompaniment to any activity involving praising classmates.

Materials:
- One 1-1/2" three-ring binder.
- Dividers with the name of each student written on the dividers.
- 5-10 sheets of paper inserted behind each divider.
- Permanent marking pen.

Book Assembly: Write the words "Compliment Book" on the cover of the binder. Insert the dividers inside the binder and write the name of a different student on each tab (dividers may be alphabetized by name). Attach a long string to one of the rings and tie a pencil to the string. Finally, insert binder paper behind each divider.

Procedure: Explain that the purpose of the Compliment Book is to increase students' awareness of one another's special attributes, then leave the book in a convenient and easily accessible location. Encourage students to take the time to write notes to one another. Notes could include questions, compliments, thank you's or needs. Emphasize that the note must be positive and may be read by any member of the class. Finally, mention to students that whenever they discover a new attribute or interest about a classmate to write it on the student's divider page. Younger students can draw their messages.

I Like Message

RS 24

Purpose: To teach students how to send respectful compliments.

Thought: *Look for strength in people, not weakness; good, not evil. Most of us find what we search for.*—Anonymous

Materials:
- I Like Message (RS24); one per student and one enlarged poster size.
- *For youngers students:* Admiral Puppet (RS1b).

Procedure: Begin by saying, "One of the nicest ways to express respect to someone is to tell them something you respect about them." Explain that there is a very specific formula anyone can use to give a respectful message or compliment. Write on the board: "I like.... + an earned quality." Ask students for the definition of a quality. Responses include:

a trait, a characteristic, something special about a person, a feature.

Next, explain that "earned" means the person already has the quality. Say, "It's not something they're trying to work on or get better at—they already are good at it! Qualities may be something you can see or something you can't see just by looking at the person, but if you get to know him or her a little better, you'd probably recognize the quality in that person."

Now invite a confident student to the front of the room and begin to describe an earned quality about the child. For younger students, use the Admiral Puppet to "admire" a trait the student possesses. Use the compliment formula as you state the quality. Here are a few examples:

> *I like Ruben's running ability.*
> *I like Zach's smile.*
> *I like Jennifer's sense of humor.*

As students become proficient in saying "I like' statements you can add another part to the compliment message: "Why do you like the trait?" This second component may be difficult for younger children. You might stick to using only the "I like" statement.

> *I like Susan's musical ability. She can play the piano well.*
> *I like Bill's hair cut. It looks great.*
> *I like Kelly's drawings. I don't know anybody else who can*
> *draw as well.*

Divide students into teams of two to four members. Give each team a copy of the "I Like Message" form. Students take turns sending "I like" compliments to one another.

For younger students: The Admiral Puppet can hand each child a 4 x 18" paper strip, pre-printed with the phrase, "I like_____." Each student can be assigned the name of another classmate. Admiral tells students they are to look for an "earned" trait they admire about the other student and then draw or print it on the line. Students may ask other students and the teacher for suggestions, but should (if possible) develop their own message.

Admiral Book/Cover   RS 25

Purpose: To increase students' respectful comments and deeds toward one another.

Thought: *I can live for two months on a good compliment.*—Mark Twain

Materials:
- Admiral Book/Cover (RS25).
- Yellow construction paper; two per student.
- Scissors and hole punch.
- 24" yarn lengths.
- Writing paper.

Procedure: Make a copy of the Admiral Book/Cover on a double piece of yellow construction paper. Cut around the shape to form the back and front cover of the book. Cut a piece of writing paper for each student from the same pattern.

Each day, choose one student to be the Admiral Book recipient of the day. Classmates draw, write or dictate respectful comments to their peers on their writing page. At the end of the day, collect all the pages and staple them between the cover. The booklet may be worn by the proud recipient by punching out the two top holes and then stringing it with a 24" piece of yarn.

Admiral Greeting Bags RS 26

Purpose: To increase respectful statements. To practice receiving compliments and respectful statements from others.

Thought: *He who gets someone else to blow his horn will find that the sound travels twice as far.*—Proverb

Materials:
- Lunch-size paper bag; one per student.
- Admiral Book/Cover (RS25); duplicated so that each student receives one from another classmate.
- Admiral Greeting (RS26); one per student.
- Glue, scissors, crayons.

Procedure: Students decorate their bags by gluing the Admiral figure to the front. Tape bags to students' desks or pin them up on a bulletin board at their eye level.

Each day choose a student (or several) to receive an Admiral Greeting from their friends. Classmates write the messages on the Admiral Greeting and insert them inside the appropriate bags. The recipients respond to the messages with verbal or written thank you's.

Pass It On! Compliments RS 27

Purpose: To practice the skill of sending and receiving compliments.

Thought: *Make the most of the best and the least of the worst.*—Robert Louis Stevenson

Materials: Pass It On Compliment (RS27); one per student duplicated on colored paper.

Procedure: Each day, choose one student to become the respectful compliment recipient. This activity is also suitable for special occasions, such as a student's birthday or a welcome back after days off for sickness. Instruct classmates to write a respectful compliment to the student using a sincere "I like" statement. Tell them they will not have enough time to read everyone's compliments. As soon as they have written a compliment and signed their name, they pass it to the next classmate until everyone has signed the form.

Receiving Compliments

RS 28

Purpose: To help students learn how to respectfully receive compliments.

Thought: *You do not have to be rich to be generous. If he has the spirit of true generosity, a pauper can give like a prince.*—Corrine V. Wells

Materials:
• Receiving Compliments (RS28); one per student and one enlarged poster size.
• Blackboard and chalk, or chart paper and colored markers.
• *For younger students:* Admiral Puppet.

Procedure: Write the word "Gratitude" on the blackboard or on chart paper and ask students to say what the word means. Responses include: appreciation, acknowledgment, gratefulness, value, recognition.

Explain that when students are given a gift of either words or a present they need to acknowledge the sender. Create a list of respectful words, phrases and statements someone can say to another to express thanks.

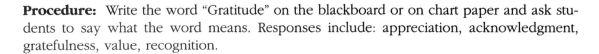

Receiving Compliments Respectfully

- Thanks!
- Thanks for noticing.
- I'm glad you like it.
- I'm pleased you think so.
- I appreciate that.
- Thank you!
- It made me feel good.
- I'm grateful.
- I'm really glad you said that.
- I'm glad you think so.
- Thank you for saying that.

Explain to students that words alone won't show their appreciation to the sender of the compliment. Posture, tone of voice, and eye contact must send the same message of gratitude. Review with students the four steps to receive a compliment. Post the Receiving Compliments poster on the board and give each student a copy of the form. To ensure students understand the four steps, divide the class into pairs to role play receiving a compliment. Students can take turns in the role of sender and receiver.

For younger students: Younger children can practice the skill of receiving compliments by role playing with Admiral and Moon Puppet. Admiral tells students: "One of the things I respect about my galaxy friends is the way they answer someone who gives them a compliment. They stand straight, look the sender in the eye, say 'thank you,' and smile. It shows the sender they like what they heard. It's the respectful way to answer a compliment. Let's practice! Someone—anyone—tell me a respectful message that makes me feel happy inside." Allow a few minutes for students to practice sending compliments to the puppet who responds to each compliment with one of the following comments: "Thanks," "Thank you," or "I appreciate that."

A Month of Respect

Purpose: To help students keep track of their own respectful actions.

Thought: *I always prefer to believe the best of everybody; it saves so much trouble.*—Anonymous

Materials: A Month of Respect (RS29); one per student.

Procedure: Instruct students to fill in the corresponding dates for the current month writing with small numbers in the upper right-hand column of the squares. At the end of each class day ask students to reflect upon what respectful things they have said or done throughout the day for themselves and for others. Students quickly note the deed they are most proud of in the corresponding box. Younger students can keep track by drawing a happy (or sad) face in the box that depicts their actions.

Compliment Stoppers

Purpose: To help students recognize disrespectful ways to receive compliments.

Thought: *Some people pay a compliment as if they expected a receipt.*—Frank Hubbard

Materials:
• Starter/Stopper Signs (RS2d and RS2e); one duplicated on red and one on green con struction paper, and cut out.
• Blackboard and chalk, or chart paper and marking pens.

Procedure: Attach the Starter and Stopper Signs to the board with double stick masking tape, or draw a large stop sign on the board. Remind students of the five ways to receive a compliment. Say, "There are stop signals you use with your body or the tone of your voice that tell the person who sent the compliment you're not appreciative of the message. These are disrespectful ways to receive a compliment." Create a T-chart on the board or chart paper and brainstorm with students disrespectful ways to receive compliments, such as the ones that follow:

COMPLIMENT STOPPERS

Sounds Like	Looks Like	

Sounds Like	Looks Like
"Who me?"	rolling eyes
"It's no big deal."	sneering
"Maybe, but..."	looking down
"Yes, but..."	ignoring the person
"You're kidding."	putting yourself down
giggling	shrugging shoulders
"Yeah, right!"	arguing
sarcasm	discounting
"Who cares?"	disowning
"So what?"	whispering
"What else is new?"	looking at the floor
	walking away
	turning around

Spraying Others with Respect   RS 31

Purpose: To practice the skill of sending and receiving compliments.

Thought: ***Those who bring sunshine to the lives of others cannot keep it from themselves.***—Sir James Barrie

Materials:
- Receiving Compliments (RS28); enlarged to poster size.
- Respectful Openers (RS14a).

Procedure: Before the end of the school day or selected class period, ask students to line up at the door in two single file lines. Select a few students who deserve recognition. As these students walk through the double lines, their classmates are to "spray them with compliments" and "well wishes" for a good day. Students may read from a list of builder-upper statements if needed. The recipients are to receive the compliments in an acceptable manner, saying, "Thank you," "I appreciate that," "Thanks for noticing," "I hope you have a great day," or any other statement listed on the Receiving Compliments Poster.

(Idea adapted from Jack Canfield and Harold Wells, *100 Ways to Enhance Self-Concept in the Classroom*, Englewood Cliffs, NJ: Prentice-Hall, 1976.)

Respectful Greeters

RS 32

Purpose: To enhance respect and courtesy through student modeling.

Thought: *Life is not so short but that there is always time enough for courtesy.*— Ralph Waldo Emerson

Materials: Per greeter: Student Greeter (RS32) duplicated on bright-colored cardstock-weight paper and ideally laminated for durability; cut along the outside margin of the sign; punch two holes at the top and string with a 24" piece of yarn.

Variations: In place of a sign, student greeters can wear caps, vests, large pins, or any other readily identifiable symbol. Ideally the attire should reflect the school colors and mascot to generate school spirit.

Procedure: *School-wide Implementation:* Clover Park School in Bremerton, Washington, recognized a gold mine in their school: students with strong social skills who can serve as models of courtesy to other students. Every school site has these students. The staff began by identifying these students and then asked them to serve in the role of Student Greeters. Special pins were made for them to wear so the students were readily identifiable. Student greeters were stationed in various locations throughout the school site to welcome their peers as well as adult visitors to the campus. For instance, each day Student Greeters met students as they walked off the bus. "Hi!," "We're glad you're here," and "Have a great day!" were the kinds of statements their peers heard as they entered the school.

The staff reported a remarkable change. At the beginning of the program, the students who were being greeted looked at the Student Greeters with disbelief. But by the end of the week, as Student Greeters continued to greet students each day, the arriving students actually started looking for the students who were there to "tell me to have a good day." The Student Greeters were modeling positive statements to students. Many of the arriving students began to return the same statements to the Student Greeters.

Student Greeters can also be trained to greet visiting parents, staff members or community officials. It's always powerful when a community member on a visit to a school is met, not by an adult, but by a student. The student welcomes the individual with a statement such as, "Welcome to our school. I know you're going to love it. We sure do. Come with me and I'll show it to you." Student Greeters can also be paired with students lacking in social skills, again, so the students can serve as models.

Classroom Adaptation: The Student Greeter activity can be adapted to individual classrooms. Appoint different students each week to serve as official Student Greeters as students walk into the classroom. To initiate the activity, the teacher should be a greeter along with the students to model proper welcoming skills. Usually by the following week students can replace the teacher as the Greeter since they've learned the skill of greeting others positively by watching.

Variation: Students can also model sending respectful compliments to peers using the formula for a respectful compliment: "I like... + an earned quality." The recipient should then turn to the sender and receive the compliment with a respectful "thank you."

Daily Greeting   RS 33

Purpose: To provide students with practice in showing the character builder of respect.

Thought: *Man lives more by affirmation than by bread.*—Victor Hugo

Materials: Daily Greeting (below); one copy per student.

Procedure: Duplicate a plentiful supply of Daily Greeting forms so they are ready for use in a number of possible ways, including:

1. Each day randomly select one student to be the Daily Greeting recipient. Each student writes (or draws) a respectful message to the designated student. Compile the completed messages into a booklet after quickly proofreading the grams to make sure each passes the "respect" criteria. Staple the pages together and present them respectfully to the students. Be sure to include your own messge.

2. Encourage students to write respectful messages to peers (or staff!) as deserving moments arise.

3. Use the forms for students to acknowledge a classmate who deserves respect on special occasions, such as a congratulation, birthday, job well done, welcome back, we're sorry, good luck, or we miss you.

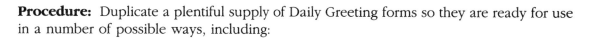

Daily Greeting

To_____

From_____

Date_____

Message

I'd like you to know_____

_____

_____

_____

_____

Remember: To get respect you must give respect!

HAVE A GREAT DAY!

Respect Literature

Purpose: To reinforce the character builder of respect through children's literature.

Thought: *There is more treasure in books than in all the pirates' loot on Treasure Island...and best of all, you can enjoy these riches every day of your life.*—Walt Disney

Materials: Any of the following books or other literature selections dealing with the concept of respect and creating a positive, respectful atmosphere.

Procedure: Choose any of the books to read aloud or to assign book reports on the theme of respect. Many teachers create a table display for the books. A colorful piece of fabric with hearts can be used over the table to place the books on.

Primary Level

Alexander and the Terrible, Horrible, No Good, Very Bad Day by Judith Viorst (Atheneum, 1972). The perfect book to keep on your shelf when the inevitable "terrible, horrible, no good, very bad day" comes to your classroom. [ALL]

A Book of Hugs by Dave Ross (Thomas Y. Crowell, 1980). This book is a wonderful catalyst for helping students to recognize that demonstrating respectful behaviors involves not only things they say to others but also things they do. [ALL]

But Names Will Never Hurt Me by Bernard Waber (Houghton Mifflin, 1976). A story about how the disrespectful actions of name-calling and teasing can hurt.

Elbert's Bad Word by Audrey Wood (Harcourt Brace Jovanovich, 1988). Young Albert snatches a "bad word" at a party and stuffs it in his pocket. Without warning, the word springs out, causing all kinds of havoc to those around him. Perplexed with his problem, he visits a wizard who tells him, "We sometimes need strong words to say how we feel," and hands Albert a few appropriate "strong words" to use. Albert discovers their miraculous impact on others.

Fortunately by Remy Charlip (Four Winds, 1987). A young boy turns every "unfortunate" into a "fortunate."

Hug Me by Patti Stren (Harper & Row, 1977). Here is a delightful little book featuring porcupines and the dilemma they face: how do you hug? Fortunately, they solve the problem.

Positively Mother Goose by Diane Loomans, Karen Kolberg and Julia Loomans (H.J. Kramer, 1991). These rhymes are a delightful twist on the traditional Mother Goose tales. The authors have turned the old rhymes into new ones that are positive, respectful and affirming. [All]

Somebody Loves You, Mr. Hatch by Eileen Spinelli (Bradbury, 1991). A year-round Valentine on the power of words and the impact respectful treatment has on others. [All]

The First Forest by John Gile (Worzalla, Stevens Point, 1989). In fable form, the author reminds us that greed and selfishness are harmful and that peace and harmony flow from an attitude of grateful appreciation for the gifts we receive and a respect for the need and right of others to share in those gifts.

The Little Brute Family by Russell Hoban (Dell). The little family of Brutes change their behavior when baby Brute brings home a happy feeling. The positive, respectful feeling is "caught" by the other family members until they recognize their last name of "Brute" is no longer appropiate. Thus, they become the "nice family."

The Quarreling Book by Charlotte Zolotow. (Harper & Row, 1963). This simple book describes a simple premise: how we treat people can have a direct impact on their actions for the rest of the day.

The Wolf's Chicken Stew by Keiko Kasza (G.P. Putnam's Sons, 1987). A hungry wolf's attempts to fatten a chicken for his pot of stew have unexpected results. The reader learns that making respectful overtures to an individual has wonderful consequences.

Intermediate Level

I'm In Charge of Celebrations by Bryd Baylor (Charles Scribner's Sons, 1986). A desert dweller celebrates a day through the wonders of the wilderness. Peter Purnall's colorful pictures illluminate the world of the desert. [M]

Slugs by David Greenberg. In lyrical form, Slug sends the message loud and clear: "Don't expect to be treated any differently than how you treat others." The story is definitely humorous—kids love it, though do make sure you familiarize yourself with it first. To some it can be offensive.

The Pushcart War by Jean Merrill (Dell, 1984). A satire based on a real incident involving the garbage strike in New York City and how negativity began to spread to all.

The Way to Start a Day by Byrd Baylor (Macmillan, 1977). This Caldecott Honor book is a beautiful way to start any day. The author describes the rituals and customs of cave-dwellers, Peruvian Indians, Egyptians and others who have celebrated the dawn.

The Whipping Boy by Sid Fleischman (Troll). This Newbery winner is the story of Prince Brat (aptly named) and Jemmy, an orphan. The tale teaches all of us about the power of kindness and how it eventually will win out.

5

Listening with Respect

KEY CONCEPTS:

- Identifying and practicing respectful listening behaviors.
- Understanding why the skill of listening is beneficial to building respect.
- Listening critically: summing up the speaker's main point.

5

Listening with Respect

The friends who listen to us are the ones we move toward,
and we want to sit in their radius.
—KARL MENNINGER

The skill of listening—or giving careful attention to the words of a speaker--is critical to students' success. Research suggests the primary way we gather new information is through listening. Without effective listening skills, children will lose the opportunity to learn valuable information. Listening is essential not only to our students' potential for success in school, but in relationships, the workplace, and the home as well. Within the family, good listening helps members stay closely bonded and keeps dissension to a minimum. Most importantly, this skill is critical in enhancing the character builder of respect. People simply love to have others really listen to them because it makes them feel cared about.

CHARACTER BUILDER STEP #4

Teach How to Listen Respectfully

While few educators would deny how important effective listening skills are to school success (as well as to self-esteem advancement), the sad but true fact is that listening is becoming a lost art in our culture. Experts in dozens of studies have verified that we listen more than any other single activity (except breathing), yet it is one of our most underdeveloped traits. The days of sitting around the family dinner table and communicating are becoming a page from the past. Our children today are being inundated with slick, high-tech visual images on the media, computer systems and video games that do little to stimulate auditory processing and interpersonal skills. One thing is for certain: educators can no longer assume that students know how to listen respectfully. Specific steps must be taken to ensure that all students are successful in demonstrating this essential life skill. The fourth step to enhancing the character builder of respect is to teach students how to listen to others.

Activities to Enhance Student Listening

The activities listed below are taken from the *Esteem Builders* series by Dr. Michele Borba.

Code	Activity	Page

A mini-session from the *Trainer's Manual* to develop staff skills in enhancing student listening.

Code	Activity	Page
F	Teaching Students to Listen	259-269

Esteem Builder Activities to help students develop listening skills. Note: Any activity in *Esteem Builders* for listening can easily be changed from an independent activity to a paired listening activity.

Code	Activity	Page
S17	Time for Friends	60
S18	Name Exchange	61
S20	Personality Trivia	61
S21	Student Interview	62
S22	Interest Search	62
S23	Find a Friend	62
S27	Secret Friendly Hello Person	63
A2	Common Points	166
A3	Getting to Know You Wheel	166
A4	Paired Name Collage	167
SW11	Name Tag Exchange	390
CC2	How Do You Do?	328
CC3	Listen Up!	328
CC4	Ball Pass	328
CC5	Partner Interview	328
CC6	Body Tracings	328
CC7	The One-Cent Interview	329

BUILDING SECURITY FOR RETICENT SPEAKERS

There are so many reasons for students' reluctance in speaking in front of others. Generally, shyness or reticent behavior in speaking is due to anxiety or insecurity in the situation. It is important to analyze the situation and ask yourself, "Have I really done everything I can to create safe parameters for this student before I require him/her to speak in front of others?" Here are a few questions to consider before beginning the speaking/listening activities:

- Do the students clearly understand the speaking (or listening) expectations?

- Did I take enough time to demonstrate the expectations?

- Are the expectations for these students appropriate? (too much or too little time? ...too large a group?...topic too difficult?).

- Have I modeled the speaking or listening behavior to students so they can "see" what I expect? Never assume students know what we are asking of them. In this day and age many of our students have never experienced the skills we are requiring of them.

- Have I provided "thinking time" before "speaking time?" Think about your own insecurity. If someone said, "You now have ten minutes to come up and start speaking on...," how secure would you feel at that moment? Impromptu speeches for students low in security are nerve-racking. Their anxiety level will be lowered if they are given time to prepare what they are going to say. Consider assigning homework the night before so that students can practice the presentation in front of a mirror, or behind a closed door, or in front of a parent. You might also consider asking students to take a moment to write on a slip of paper the "the three most important points you want to remember to say." In this way, students learn to organize their thoughts and may refer to the card when they are ready to speak.

- Have I provided a safe environment for students to speak? Does the audience (or stu--dent's partner) know what is required? Audiences should know that absolutely no talking is allowed while someone is speaking. The presentation should be followed by praise or applause.

- Did I provide "safer partners" for reticent speakers? Students low in security need safer partners; they do not need balantly over-confident partners who exude self-confidence! Such partners only shatter the confidence of students low in security. It is critical to plan ahead for these students and deliberately pair them with more "merciful students."

- Is the speaking time appropriate for these students? It is always better to start listening and speaking experiences with short time limits. Thirty seconds is fine to begin. Gradually increase the speaking time as students' security grows.

> "He has the right to criticize who has the heart to help."
>
> —Abraham Lincoln

SAFER LISTENING PARTNERS

Pairing students up for the first paired activity should never happen by chance. Students low in security, in particular, often have a very difficult time in partner sharing activities because they are not risk-takers and have a difficult time managing change. For this reason, educators must plan who to pair such students with. The following is a list of possible "safer" partners for students lower in security:

- *More Compassionate Students*. These students are generally more tolerant and more merciful toward students low in security.

- *Cross-Age Tutors*. Students a grade level or more above the grade level of students low in security can be trained to serve as partners a few times each week or month. It is critical to first train the cross-age tutors as to your expectations.

- *Parent Aides*. Parents may be able to donate time on a regular basis to serve as social mentors to students.

- *Same Sex Partners*. Particularly with young adolescents, partners of the same sex are safer for students low in security.

- *Younger Students*. For non-participating or shyer students, try younger or quieter students. Shyer students don't always need verbal, overly-confident partners, but instead may need the opportunity to practice skills with younger, and perhaps more accepting, students.

- *The Teacher*. It's always a possibility that the teacher may be the only alternative. For students who desperately need an accepting partner to practice new behaviors with, the teacher may be the only person for a while who is that accepting.

Teacher Tip: Students low in security are often quite uncomfortable using eye contact with their partners. A simple "tension reliever" is to privately tell reticent students to "look at the bridge of your partner's nose" instead of their eyes. It's amazing how less threatened they will feel and how soon the students build enough security to actually look in their partner's eyes.

"The best way to cheer yourself up is to try to cheer somebody else up."
—Mark Twain

PARTNER SHARING

In Partner Sharing, students are paired with partners to take turns listening to one another share ideas on an assigned topic. One student is assigned the role of the "listener" and the other student is given the role of the "speaker" or "sharer." At the end of a short set time, students exchange roles and resume sharing on the assigned topic.

This simple cooperative learning structure is based on the work of Spencer Kegan and Frank Lyman and has limitless possibilities for classroom work. Here are just a few:

- *Greeting.* Each day students are required to turn to their partners and greet or "affirm" them while practicing the behavior of respectful listening. Greeting topics the teacher might suggest include:

  Ask your partner what they are looking forward to doing today.
  Find out one thing your partner did last night.
  What is your partner planning to do this weekend?
  Greet your partner with a sincere hello.

- *Homework Exchange.* Student partners can quickly exchange homework papers to compare learning or establish if they reached similar conclusions.

- *Partner Prediction.* Before finishing a story or text, students can quickly predict with their partners what they think the outcome will be.

- *Oral Reading.* Partners can take turns listening to one another read aloud from assigned or chosen passages.

- *Oral Book Report.* Partners listen respectfully to one another describing what they just read in a literature selection.

- *Summarizer.* Partners briefly summarize the main idea or key facts from their independent reading.

Possible topics for students to speak about in shared partner activities are endless. Here are a few pointers to think about to ensure that your initial sessions are successful:

1. Student Choice. Set aside a small box with a pencil and scratch paper. Label the box "Topics for Sharing." Encourage students to suggest possible speaking topics. You'll want to read suggested student topics ahead of time. Periodically drop in a few anonymous suggestions of your own so students can get an idea of successful topic choices.

2. Brief Speaking Times. Borrow a stop watch and then use it! Beginning Partner Sharing activities should be no more than one minute of sharing per student. Gradually increase the speaker's time when you see students' security increasing.

3. Non-threatening Topics. Beginning topics should be non-threatening. Children don't feel secure talking about "my greatest strengths and attributes" as a beginning topic. Choose "safer" topics students will feel comfortable sharing.

4. "Kid Relevant." Students love to talk about themselves, so why not use "students" as your sharing motif? Find out what your students like to do (skateboarding, rock groups, favorite TV shows, etc.) and incorporate their interests into the topics for sharing.

5. Post the Listening Chart. Keep the chart posted as a visual reminder to students of effective listening behaviors. You'll find students "sneaking a glance" to copy down the behaviors more than you'd ever think. Most students are not comfortable demonstrating listening skills because they simply have not had enough quality practice opportunities to "do it right." Provide them with the opportunities.

Teacher Tip: The skill of eye contact needs to be practiced frequently. A simple technique is to use the skill throughout the day by making a rule that anytime anyone is speaking (student or teacher) "all eyes are on the speaker." Explain the rule once and from then on merely say "eyes on speaker" as a reminder for students to practice the skill.

Respectful Listening

RS 35

Purpose: To teach students what respectful listening "looks like" and "sounds like."

Thought: *There is only one rule for being a good communicator: learn to listen.—* Christopher Morley

Materials:
- Listening (RS47); enlarged poster size.
- Looks Like/Sounds Like (RS1d); one per student.
- Blackboard and chalk, or chart paper and colored markers.

For younger students:
- Eye/Ear Images (RS1f and RS1g); one per student and one enlarged poster size.
- Admiral Puppet (RS1b).

Procedure: Gather students to a Class Meeting and introduce the Listening Poster. Explain the definition of respectful listening as, "Showing consideration and careful attention to the words and feelings of a speaker." Emphasize how critical this skill is for students' success in school, with friends, in getting a job, and in life!

Ask one student (or another staff member) to come forward and stand with you at the front of the room. (Note: Choose a student who is confident in front of groups, generally willing to take risks, and high in security.) Tell students their job in the next few minutes is to watch you and not the speaker. You will show students what respectful listening "looks like" and "sounds like."

Invite the chosen student to tell you anything he/she did before coming to school today that is appropriate and that he/she would like to share. Explain that the student does not need to talk for more than a minute, but everyone in the room will know by your behavior you've been respectfully listening to the student. (Another student could time the conversation so that the listening activity does not extend beyond one minute.)

Your role now is to demonstrate to the students what listening behaviors look like. The actual activity should take no more than a minute. Turn the student toward you so that the two of you are standing face to face. The two of you should then be standing sideways to the group so that the group sees only your outside shoulders. Ask the student to describe what he/she did that morning before arriving at school. Once the speaker begins, you should not say anything except "uh huh" or "yes." Your job is to convey good, respectful listening behaviors, such as facing the speaker squarely at all times, raising your eyebrows at key points, smiling and nodding, appearing animated and enthused, leaning forward slightly, looking directly into his/her eyes, keeping your arms by your side, and not interrupting.

At the end of the minute thank the student and tell the rest of the students to give the child a big hand.

On the blackboard or on chart paper draw a large T-chart that covers the full space of the medium you are working with. Write the words "Respectful Listening" at the top of the paper. On the left side of the T write "Looks Like" and on the right of the T write "Sounds Like." For younger students, either the teacher or the Admiral puppet can tape up the eye and ear images.

Now remind students you just demonstrated the skill of respectful listening. Ask students to tell you specifically what they saw you do that showed them you were listening to the student. Say, "Remember, I want you to tell me only what you saw me do. At this point I do not want you to tell me what you heard me say. What you saw me do is called 'Looks Like.'" List the students' ideas under the "Looks Like" side of the chart, or under the eye image. Continually remind students to be very specific.

When a list has been obtained, ask students to now refer to the "Sounds Like" side of the chart, or the ear image. Emphasize that you deliberately did not say much during the activity other than "uh huh" and "yes." Explain that as students practice the skill of listening, they will be learning kinds of statements they can say to the speaker to show they are listening. A completed group chart might look like this:

 RESPECTFUL LISTENING

Looks Like	**Sounds Like**
nodding	"yes"
smiling	no interrupting
eye to eye	sincere voice
waiting patiently	
leaning in	
sitting square	
face to face	
feet flat	
raising eyebrows	
hands in lap	

Provide students with a "Looks Like/Sounds Like" form. Working with their partners, students copy the chart completed by the group on their own papers and then file them in their Character Builder Notebooks.

Teacher Tip: Be aware of your students' cultural backgrounds and the skills deemed "appropriate and inappropriate." In some cultures, children making eye contact to an adult (or even another student) is considered "disrespectful." Do accept cultural differences by adapting skills to meet their needs and show respect for their culture.

Listening Body Tracing `RS 36`

Purpose: To increase younger students' awareness of the total body behaviors needed for respectful listening.

Thought: *It takes two to speak truth--one to speak and another to hear.*—Henry David Thoreau

Materials: Butcher paper or brown wrapping paper; marking pens.

Procedure: Each student lies down on a piece of butcher paper or brown wrapping paper while a classmate draws around his/her body. Working with their partners, students label respectful listening behaviors in the appropriate locations within the body outline. Responses might include: mouth, shut while speaker is speaking; lips, smiling; eyes, on speaker's face; feet, flat on floor and still; neck, nodding as speaker talks; shoulders, leaning in towards speaker; hands, lying still in lap.

Students can then color or paint their self pictures to look like they do today, using a mirror to check the details of clothing and physical characteristics.

Listening Hats `RS 37`

Purpose: To help younger students gain an awareness of the benefits of listening as a respect builder.

Thought: *Give every man thy ear, but few thy voice.*—William Shakespeare

Literature Link: *The Cat Who Wore A Pot On Her Head* by Jan Slepain and Ann Seidler (Scholastic, 1980). This humorous gem depicts a kitten who always seems to mix up directions and listen incorrectly because of the pot she wears on her head. It isn't until she takes the pot off her head and tunes into what people are saying that "life becomes fun again." This book is particularly fun to use with young children.

Materials: Per student: lunch-size paper bag, scissors, stapler, 2 x 8" strip of black construction paper.

Procedure: Share the story with students and discuss the benefits of learning to listen. Ask, "What did the kitten learn about the need to listen carefully? What message does walking away from a speaker send to him or her? What happens when we don't listen carefully? How can we show the speaker we respect what he or she is saying?"

Extension Activity: Students can make "pot hats" to wear just like the kitten in the story. Fold a medium-size paper bag a few inches from the top to "pot size." Staple a black construction paper handle (cut 8 x 2") to one side of the pot. Students enjoy retelling the story with partners by wearing the paper pot and then taking it off just in time to solve their listening dilemma.

Partner Sharing
RS 38

Purpose: To provide a structured opportunity for students to practice the behavior of listening respectfully. To help students talk about their ideas and hear the ideas of others.

Thought: *An open ear is the only believable sign of an open heart.*—David Augsburger

Materials:
- Partner Sharing (RS38); one copy per student and one enlarged poster size.
- Starter and Stopper Signs (RSd and RS2e); one copy duplicated on red and one on green construction paper.
- Masking tape and scissors.
- Blackboard and chalk, or chart paper and marking pens.

Procedure: Begin the activity by briefly reviewing good listening skills. Draw a T-chart on the blackboard or on chart paper and ask students what good listening "looks like" and "doesn't look like." Tape the starter (go sign) above the "looks like" section of the T and stopper (stop sign) above the "doesn't look like" section. Write students' ideas on the board as a visual reminder of your expectations for good listening.

 **RESPECTFUL LISTENING**

Starters	**Stoppers**
Looks Like	**Doesn't Look Like**
Nodding head.	Snarling.
Smiling.	Smirking.
Eye to eye.	Rolling eyes.
One speaker at a time.	Interrupting.
12" voice.	Shouting.
Feet on floor.	Walking away.
Sitting square.	Turning around.
Hands in lap.	Messing with something.
Interested tone.	Sarcastic tone.

Next choose any of the Partner Sharing Topics on the next page or another of your choice. Write the topic on the board or on chart paper and say it to students. Review the Partner Sharing activity with students taking a few minutes for students to role play the listener and speaker parts.

Finally, ask students to use the Partner Sharing Topic for the day to actually do Partner Sharing. Tell students the person in the pair who has the longest hair will be the speaker while the person with the shortest hair will be the listener. Speakers are to continue talking on the topic until you say "time" (to begin, provide no more than one minute). Students then freeze and reverse roles.

Following the activity briefly describe a few students who demonstrated respectful listening. Tell the rest of the group the exact behaviors you saw these students performing which told you they were listening respectfully. A few minutes of specifically reinforcing respectful listeners will remind the rest of the students about the kinds of behaviors they should be practicing.

"Practice courtesy. You never know when it might become popular again."
—Bill Copeland

Partner Sharing Topics

- What is your favorite movie?
- What is your favorite television show?
- Tell me two things you really like to do.
- What do you do on a typical Saturday afternoon?
- What is your favorite book?
- What is your favorite music group...instrument...rock group?
- What is your favorite pet and why?
- What is your favorite food....pizza topping, ice cream flavor?
- Tell me about things you like.
- Describe a moment you'll never forget.
- I know a person is listening to me when...
- Quickly tell the plot of a book you've read recently.
- Describe a character you're reading about.
- Retell the directions for a classroom activity.
- Describe your partner's best traits.
- Describe a room in your home.
- Describe your favorite holiday.
- Tell about a scary experience.
- Share the recipe for any meal.
- Five years from now...
- One hundred years from now...
- If I could be a CD I'd be...because...
- If I could be any famous person I'd be...because...
- If I could meet any famous person I'd like to meet...because...
- I like people who...
- What kids really need that grown-ups don't give us is...
- I wish...
- Three things I want to become more of are...
- Three adjectives that best describe me are...
- I'm happiest when...
- The most exciting thing that's happened to me this week...this year...is...
- The one skill I wish everyone would learn is...
- The one thing that would make the world a better place is...
- I spend most of my free time by...
- The three qualities I admire most in grown-ups are...
- The three qualities I admire least in people are....
- One thing I'm looking forward to is...
- When I grow up, I want to...
- If I had a choice on how to make the world a better place, it would be...
- Tomorrow I'd like to...

Respectful Listening Quotations RS 39

Purpose: To help students recognize how listening enhances the character builder of respect; to provide the opportunity for students to practice respectful listening.

Thought: *There is only one rule for being a good talker—learn how to listen.*—Christopher Morley

Materials:
For older students:
• Partner Sharing (RS38); enlarged poster size.
• Respectful Thoughts (RS11b); one per student.
• Blackboard and chalk, or chart paper and marking pens.

Procedure: Each day for the next fifteen days set aside five minutes to practice structured paired sharing. Write on the blackboard or chart paper one of the quotations provided below about the value of listening, or another selection of your choice. Ask students to think about the thought and then take turns describing to their partners in one minute what they think its author meant. Following the two minute sharing (one minute per student) invite a few students to share either their thought or their partners' thoughts.

The activity can be extended to a written activity by having students copy the quotation on the Respectful Thoughts form followed by their interpretation. Invite students to bring in additional quotations about the topic of listening to use in the activity.

• "Half the world is composed of people who have something to say and can't, and the other half who have nothing to say and keep on saying it"—Robert Frost.

• "The communicator is the person who can make himself clear to himself first."—Paul D. Griffith

• "You can have brilliant ideas, but if you can't get them across, your ideas won't get you anywhere."—Lee Iacocca

• "The friends who listen to us are the ones we move toward, and we want to sit in their radius."—Karl Menninger

• "A single conversation across the table with a wise man is better than a ten-year study of books."—Henry Wadsworth Longfellow

• I believe I shall never be old enough to speak without embarrassment when I have nothing to talk about."—Abraham Lincoln

• "It is better to remain quiet and be thought a fool than to speak and remove all doubt."—Anonymous

• "When people talk, listen completely. Most people never listen."—Ernest Hemingway

- "From listening comes wisdom, and from speaking repentance."—Italian proverb

- "He understands badly who listens badly."—Welsh proverb

- "Know how to listen, and you will profit even more than those who talk badly."—Plutarch

- "One of the best ways to persuade others is with your ears—by listening to them."—Dean Rusk

- "There is only one rule for being a good talker—learn how to listen."—Christopher Morley

- "While the right to talk may be the beginning of freedom, the necessity of listening is what makes the right important."—Walter Lippmann

- "You can't fake listening. It shows."—Raquel Welch

Spoke Graph   RS 40

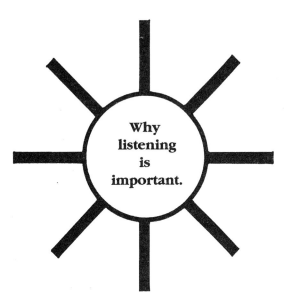

Purpose: To help students recognize the value of listening as a life skill for success not only in school and relationships but also to enhance respect.

Thought: *A good listener is not only popular everywhere but after a while he knows something.*—Wilson Mizner.

Materials:
- Partner Sharing (RS38); enlarged poster size.
- Chart paper and marking pens, or blackboard and chalk

Procedure: Call students to a Class Meeting. On the blackboard or chart paper draw a large circle with 8-15 "spokes" (lines about 12 inches in length) starting from the edge of the circle to the end of the chart. Tell students this is called a "Spoke Graph" and is used to "organize ideas." Explain that today's meeting is to discuss "why listening is an important skill to learn."

Ask students to quickly form partners. Review the Partner Sharing rules. Explain that each partner will share a reason why they think listening is a valuable skill to learn. Students take turns sharing ideas for one minute each using the rules of Partner Sharing.

Review the rules of brainstorming. Explain you want to hear different reasons why listening is an important skill to learn. Tell students they may share their own ideas or their partners' ideas that were mentioned during Partner Sharing. Now ask, "How can listening help you in school? at home? on the playground? with friends? even when you're older?" or "How does good listening skills build respect?" Write each different response on a "spoke." Benefits from learning the skill of listening might include:

- Reduces conflict.
- Helps you get friends.
- Saves you from getting in trouble.
- Improves your grades.
- Helps you get a job.
- Helps you find out what you need.
- Helps you understand how someone feels.
- For enjoyment!
- Understand what someone needs.
- Learn how to do something.
- Learn new ideas.

Finally, ask students to work with their partners to make a copy of the Spoke Graph and then file it in their Character Builder Notebook.

Companion Reading   RS 41

Purpose: To practice the skills of effective listening and respectful attitude through oral reading.

Thought: *The tongue is the only tool that gets sharper with use.*—Washington Irving.

Materials:
- Companion Reading (RS41); enlarged poster size.
- Sending Compliments (RS22); enlarged poster size
- Reading books (texts and/or literature) suitable to the reading levels of each student; one book per student.
- Blackboard and chalk, or chart paper and marking pens.

Procedure: Call students to a Class Meeting and describe the structured activity called "Companion Reading" where partners take turns reading aloud to one another. Establish a specific reading time, ideally at the same time each day, and assign students a Reading Companion. For management ease, students can keep the same partners for a minimum of one week. Specify the time each partner is to read aloud, generally three to ten minutes per reader. The length will depend on the students' age and abilities. Tell students that as the "time keeper," you will let students know when to switch from being reader to listener by simply saying, "Switch." Write the three rules of a good reading companion on the blackboard or chart—Listen, Check, Encourage—and explain them to students:

1. Listen Respectfully. Tell students they are to practice listening skills with their partners just as they do in Partner Sharing. This time their partners will be sharing their reading. Review the rules of respectful listening: "No interrupting, eye to eye, smiling, leaning in, and nodding."

"Nothing is more becoming in a great man than courtesy and forbearance."
—Cicero

2. Check. Explain that if readers are stuck on a word, they are to figure it out together with their companions. First allow partners time to see if they can figure out the word themselves. If they need help, offer it. If both partners need help, turn to another pair of Companion Readers.

3. Encourage. Reading companions should send at least two respectful "put-up" statements to their partners. One put-up is said while their partners are reading, the second put-up is said when partners are finished reading. Tell students they may choose put-ups from the Put Up chart, if needed.

Students then reverse roles so that readers now become listeners, checkers and encouragers. *(Idea from William F. Davidson School in Surrey, B.C.)*

School-Wide Idea: I've often seen Companion Reading implemented school-wide. Imagine walking down school halls at ten o'clock on any morning and seeing dozens of students reading together as companions while practicing respectful listening and respectful attitude. It's always an impressive sight.

Partner Recall

Purpose: To enhance students' ability to recall a speaker's message and show respect by conveying they understood the message.

Thought: *It is the province of knowledge to speak, and it is the privilege of wisdom to listen.*—Oliver Wendell Holmes, Jr.

Materials:
• Partner Recall (RS42); one copy per student and one enlarged poster size.
• Any Partner Sharing Topic; personal or subject-related (page 103).

Teacher Tip: Younger children often have a difficult time waiting for their turn to speak.

Role Cards are a simple reminder to help students remember their roles as speaker or listener. You'll need two pieces of 4 x 8' cardstock-weight paper folded in half per Partner Sharing team. Using colored markers, draw lips on one card and ears on the other. In the Partner Sharing activity described below, speakers will hold the "lips" card and listeners will hold the "ears" card so that everyone can instantly see who are the real speakers and listeners.

It takes repeated practice for students to model the correct behaviors associated with effective listening (eye contact, nodding, sitting square, leaning in, etc.). In the initial stages of teaching the skills of listening, do not assume that students are capable of processing what their partner has said. Generally, beginning listeners (at any age!) need repeated opportunities to practice listening behaviors before they are ready to repeat back the speaker's words. The following activities help students learn the second step of listening: paraphrasing or recalling the message of the partner. In this stage the listener recalls what he heard the speaker say almost word by word.

Showing A Speaker You Understand

- "One thing I heard you say was..."
- "One thing that interested me was..."
- "I remember you said..."
- "I want to know more about..."
- "Two things I heard you say were..."
- "Three things I heard you say were..."
- "I understand. You said..."
- "I see."
- "I don't understand..."
- "Would you say that again please?"

Procedure: Explain that one way to be a respectful listener is to show the speaker you understand what he or she just said. Write the word "paraphrase" (with younger children use the term "recall") on the blackboard or chart paper. Ask for meanings of the term. Responses include: giving back exactly what you heard, remembering, telling back what the speaker said.

Introduce the Partner Recall poster and activity to students. Tell students that Partner Recall is the same as Partner Sharing. Each person takes turns sharing their idea to their partner. Partner Recall does one thing more than Partner Sharing: after the speakers are finished sharing, the listeners let the speakers know they understood what they just said.

Explain that there are many ways to do this. Say, "I'm going to tell you something I did last night. When I'm done, I want you somehow to let me know you understood what I said." In a minute or less describe to students any event you did last night. When finished, ask, "Someone tell me you understood what I said."

Write on a chart or blackboard: "Showing a Speaker You Understand." Guide students into simply paraphrasing your words. Fill in statements that could be used by any listener and create a chart. Students can refer to the chart to find ways to show speakers they understand (or didn't understand) their message. Tell students to try to remember at least one thing the speaker said. Suggest listeners write down a "key word" on a piece of paper while the speakers are talking so they won't forget. Now divide students into pairs and designate the first speakers for each partnership.

Quick Teacher Tips:
• *Quicken the Pace.* Whenever you notice an energy ebb, you can revitalize the pace by using Partner Sharing. Say, "Turn to your partner and tell one fact you just heard." This can add instant energy to the classroom.

• *Summarize.* Ask students to work with their partners and come up with a paragraph that summarizes the main ideas in the lecture.

• *A Chance to Be Heard.* With growing class sizes, it's hard to hear everyone's ideas. Students quickly learn: "Why bother?" Here's an opportunity for everyone to quickly "turn to your partner and share your idea."

• *Personalize the Content.* "Turn to your partner and share a time you've had the same kind of feeling as the character."

• *Increase Attentiveness.* "Listen carefully. I'll stop every two minutes and ask you to turn to your partner and recall what you just heard."

• *Share Opinions.* "You may agree or disagree about the effectiveness of the boycott on Cuba. Please pair up and share your opinion on President Kennedy's decision."

• *Give Meaning to Content.* Students put key thoughts they heard in their own words.

Paraphrase Ticket   RS 43

Purpose: To teach students to "speak in turn" and listen respectfully to the words of the previous speaker.

Thought: *The road to the heart is the ear.*—Voltaire

Materials:
• Partner Recall (RS42); enlarged poster size.
• Per team: 3 x 5" piece of colored construction paper.
• Any Partner Sharing Topic; personal or subject-related.

Procedure: Write the word "paraphrase" (younger children use the term "recall") on the blackboard or chart paper. Ask for meanings of the term. Responses include: giving back exactly what you heard, remembering, restating what the speaker said.

Now divide students in partners (or quads). Hand the speakers a piece of paper and tell them it is "a ticket to speak." The first speakers will talk on the topic and then hand the "talking ticket" to their partners. The partners must first paraphrase/tell back/recall a few words or thoughts from the speakers before sharing their own ideas on the topic. Write the rules on the blackboard or chart paper:

1. Take the ticket.
2. Paraphrase.
3. Share.
4. Pass the ticket.

Teacher Tip: Use ticket paraphrasing for any class discussion. The rule simply is: "You may not share your idea until you have quickly restated the idea of the previous speaker." The rule instantly improves students' listening attention.

Interested Listener Comments   RS 44

Purpose: To increase students' awareness of the kinds of statements listeners say to enhance respectful communication.

Thought: *There is nothing so frustrating as a person who keeps right on talking while I'm trying to interrupt.*—Anonymous

Materials:
- Blackboard and chalk, or chart paper and marking pens; or the student-created paper-body outlines from the Listening Body Tracing activity.
- Chart paper and marking pens and scissors, or tagboard pre-cut into sentence strips (4 x 16" for younger students; 1 x 8" for older students).

For older students:
- Interested Listener Comments (RS44a); one per each student Partner Sharing team to store in their Character Builder Notebooks.

For younger students:
- I Said/You Said (RS44b); one per student.

Procedure: As students become more proficient in acquiring respectful listening behaviors, teach Partner Sharing teams sentence stems that can be used at the conclusion of the listening activity. These can become part of an ongoing chart of Listening Stems. Team members can also quickly fill in a summary of what they heard their partners say on the "I Said/You Said" form.

Ask students to think of statements listeners could say to speakers to show they are interested in what was said. Tell students these are called "Interested Listener Responses." Write responses on chart paper or on phrase cards for younger students. Explain that respectful listeners often use comments such as these to let the speaker know they are interested in what the speaker is saying. Pass out a copy of the Interested Listener Responses for older students. For younger students, choose only one of the phrases to place on the blackboard.

Divide students into pairs and assign any Partner Sharing Topic (page 103). Tell students each person in the pair will have the opportunity to be the speaker and the listener. Following each speaking time (no more than three minutes) explain that listeners must say back the Interested Listener Responses. Older students can evaluate the effectiveness of the comment in the space on the form marked evaluation with either a happy or sad face, a short written description (effective, ineffective) or even a code number (1 = effective, 3 = ineffective) and store the form in their notebooks.

There are dozens of ways to use quick partner sharing ideas with your students. Here are just a few options that don't take any more than one minute.

- *Direction Agreement.* Turn to a partner and reach an agreement as to the task directions.

- *Partner Affirmation.* Turn to a partner and say, "Good Morning," or "Good Job." Ask about last night. Ask if he/she has any questions.

- *Homework Check.* Discuss with a partner three facts from last night's homework.

- *Create a List.* Create a list of things of: mammal characteristics, nouns, numbers divisible by 2, adjectives, things on a farm, things on a prairie, words starting with B, contractions.

- *Practice Rules.* Recite the rules: of the class, geometry, volleyball, adjectives, nouns.

- Geographic Locations. Take out a map and with a partner find these locations.

- *Quick Paper Exchange.* You have 30 seconds to exchange papers. Read your partner's work and either: find one error and correct it, or find one thing your partner did well and support him/her.

- *Writing Ideas.* Take 30 seconds to turn to a partner and brainstorm ideas to use in an essay.

- *Physical Education Drills.* Practice the drill just learned with a partner.

- *Support.* Help a partner organize his/her notebook, desk, portfolio.

- *Goals.* Look through a partner's portfolio and identify one goal that would help him/her improve in his/her work task.

- *Problem Solving.* Tell the problem to a partner and see if he/she can solve it before telling it to the teacher.

- *Practice Test.* Give partner a practice test on spelling words, rules to a game, math facts, geographic locations.

"Life is not so short but that there is always time enough for courtesy."
—Emerson

• *Absences.* If partner is absent, take a moment to make a get well card for him/her. Gather all assignments together to hand to the partner when he/she returns.

• *Research.* As quickly as possible, work with a partner to look up one fact about...the definition of...the location of...a main characteristic of....

Listener Scorecard   `RS 45`

Purpose: To practice the skill of respectful listening.

Thought: ***Two great talkers will not travel far together.***--Spanish Proverb

Materials: Respectful Listener Scorecard (RS45a) for older students; (RS45b) for younger students.

Procedure: Assign a daily topic for Partner Sharing, either personal or content-based. Explain that following each Partner Sharing session, students will evaluate their listening performance on the card, and write one goal of what they will do next time to improve their respectful listening skills.

Books on Listening   `RS 46`

Purpose: To gain an awareness of the importance of learning the character builder skill of listening.

Thought: ***When I get a little money, I buy books; and if any is left, I buy food and clothes.***—Desiderius Erasmus

Materials: One or more books from the list below appropriate to grade level. Either read aloud or assign as independent reading.

Primary Level

The Conversation Club by Diane Stanley (Macmillan, 1983). Overwhelmed by his friends' Conversation Club where each member speaks at the same time, Peter Fieldmouse forms a Listening Club.

The Talking Earth by Jean George Craighead (Harper, 1983). Billie Wind ventures out alone into the Everglades to test the legends of her Indian ancestors and learns the importance of listening to the earth's vital messages.

What Do You Do When Your Mouth Won't Open? by Susan Beth Pfeffer (Dell, 1981). Eighth grader Reesa has just won an essay contest at her school which she must now deliver in a speech. Her problem is a severe fear of speaking in front of others. This book is packed with effective ways to reduce such fears as well as actual tools to enhance public speaking. [M-A]

The Shrinking of Treehorn by Florence Parry Heide (Holiday House, 1971). A young boy tries to tell everyone he is shrinking but everyone ignores him. Sequel: Treehorn's Treasure. [M]

Stringbean's Trip to the Shining Sea by Vera B. Williams. The entire book is laid out like postcards!

The Important Book by Margaret Wise Brown (Harper Trophy, 1991). This book has become a teacher's classic because of its countless classroom applications. Each page in the picture book contains a repetitive paragraph that students can instantly grab onto as a model for writing or speaking. [ALL]

Nobody Listens to Andrew by Elizabeth Guilfoile (Scholastic, 1967). This classic has been around for years and is still a gem. Andrew tries to tell everyone there is a bear in his bed. The problem is no one listens. The outcome is predictable (there really is a bear in Andrew's bed) and the discussion possibilities with children are endless ("Have you ever felt like Andrew where no one listens?")

I Hate English! by Ellen Levine (Scholastic, 1989). When her family moves to New York from Hong Kong, Mei Mei finds it difficult to adjust to school and learn the alien sounds of English. It takes a special teacher to help her feel comfortable. [P]

Crow Boy by Taro Yashima (Scholastic, 1983). A small, shy boy is isolated by his differences from other children in the village. The gift of a special teacher helps Chibi identify his strengths and teaches others to treat him with the specialness he deserves. [P]

The Way it Happened by Deborah Zemke (Houghton Mifflin Co., 1988). Here is the classic story of how rumors can start and blow way out of proportion if no one listens. When Sarah falls from her bicycle, each character relays to the next person what happened until humorous results transpire. [P]

Even That Moose Won't Listen to Me by Martha Alexander (Dial, 1988). A little girl tries various means to get rid of a giant moose in the garden after she repeatedly warns her family and they refuse to listen to her. [P]

Sister Yessa's Story by Karen Greenfield and Claire Ewart (Harper Collins, 1992). Dark clouds gather as Yessa walks to her brother's place, telling a story as she goes about the early days of the earth. The animals follow her two by two to listen.

The 329th Friend by Marjorie Winman Sharmat (Four Winds, 1979). Bored with his own company, Emery Raccoon invites 328 guests to lunch but finds that none of them have time to listen to him.

The Cat Who Wore A Pot On Her Head by Jan Slepain and Ann Seidler (Scholastic, 1980). This humorous gem depicts a kitten who always seems to mix up directions and listens incorrectly because of the pot she wears on her head. It isn't until she takes the pot off her head and tunes into what people are saying that "life becomes fun again."

Puppets

Please refer to pages 17-21, "How to use Character Builder Puppets," for ways to use the puppet images.

Admiral the Moon

Permisssion to reprint for classroom use.
Character Builders, Jalmar Press
© 2001 by Michele Borba

BURNER RS18

Worksheets, Activities, and Posters

CARING

RESPONSIBILITY

CHARACTER BUILDER NOTEBOOK

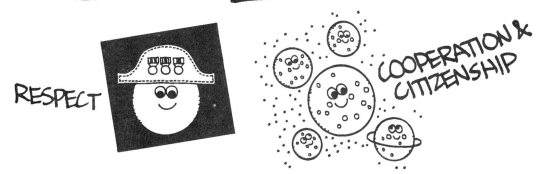

RESPECT

COOPERATION & CITIZENSHIP

PROPERTY OF

_____

YEAR _____

RS1c

Respect

**Treating others in a courteous, considerate
and polite manner.
Valuing yourself and others.**

Looks Like	Sounds Like

RESPECT RULE: Before you say anything, ask yourself:
    "Is it Kind?" and "Is it necessary?"

RESPECT MOTTO: "Give respect to get respect."

Name _____ **Date** _____

Today's Topic: _____

What I think:

How I Feel:

RS1e

LOOKS LIKE

RS1f

SOUNDS LIKE

RS1g

FEELS LIKE

STOPPERS AND STARTERS

Character Builder: Respect:
"To get respect you must give respect."

RESPECT: Treating others in a courteous, considerate and polite manner.
Valuing yourself and others.

RS2a

Name _____ Date _____

DISRESPECTFUL PICTURES

RS2c

RS2d

RS2e

A Month of Respect

1. Number the days for this month.   2. Use these ideas as a guide for your daily journal writing.

MONDAY	TUESDAY	WEDNESDAY	THURSDAY	FRIDAY
Give a sincere compliment to someone.	Look up the definition of respect.	Make a list of people you think are respectful.	Think of someone who is respectful and talk about why they would be a good friend.	Discuss why acting respectful is important.
What are three ways you can show your teacher respect?	What are three ways you can show your parents respect?	Watch a half hour TV show. Who was respectful or disrespectful, and why?	Interview someone and ask what's one way to show respect to another person.	List five ways we could show greater respect for our environment.
Describe a respectful way to answer the phone.	Read about John Muir. How did he show respect to the environment?	List at least five synonyms for the word respect.	Cut out a newspaper or magazine article about a person who showed respect. What did they do?	Write a word for each letter in the word respect that means almost the same thing.
List five antonyms for the word respect.	Find at least five pictures of people showing respect to others. Make a collage.	Write a paragraph describing how the world would be different if more people showed respect toward one another.	Create a recipe for respect. What do you need?	Design a campaign button for respect.

Permission to reprint for classroom use.
Character Builders, Jalmar Press
© 2001 by Michele Borba

RESPECT PLEDGE

I pledge to the best of my ability to uphold the basic human rights of treating everyone in the classroom, school and world in the same way I would like to be treated—respectfully!

Respect Rule: Before you say anything, ask yourself: "Is it kind?" and "Is it necessary?"

Signed _____

Witness _____

Dated _____

Respect Motto: To get respect you must give respect.

RESPECT BOOKMARKS
To get respect, you must give respect.

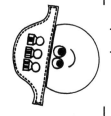

Reputable

Name: _____

Date: _____

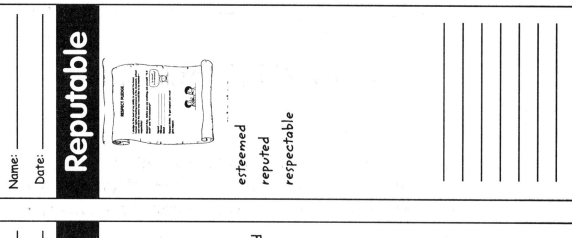

esteemed
reputed
respectable

Decent

Name: _____

Date: _____

Next time I get upset, I will be more tolerable of others.

acceptable   aboveboard
adequate   right
all right
good
satisfactory
sufficient
tolerable

Honest

Name: _____

Date: _____

DO I NEED TO APOLOGIZE?

credible   fair
praiseworthy   sincere
respectable   upright
aboveboard   honorable
reputable   genuine
well thought of
honorable
trustworthy

Respect

Name: _____

Date: _____

I appreciate what you do.

admire   appreciate
regard   embrace
adulate   approve
adore
venerate
honor
esteem
revere

RS8

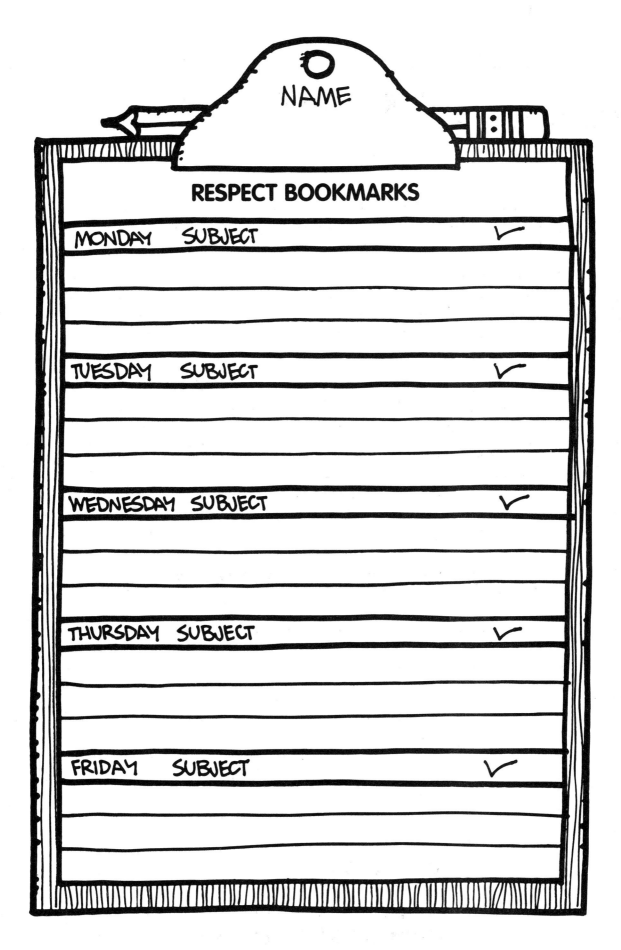

NAME

RESPECT BOOKMARKS

MONDAY   SUBJECT   ✓

TUESDAY   SUBJECT   ✓

WEDNESDAY   SUBJECT   ✓

THURSDAY   SUBJECT   ✓

FRIDAY   SUBJECT   ✓

Name_____ **Date** _____

A THOUGHT FOR THE DAY

Today's Date _____   Today's Thought_____
_____
_____

My thoughts and ideas _____
_____
_____
_____

Today's Date _____   Today's Thought_____
_____
_____

My thoughts and ideas _____
_____
_____
_____

Today's Date _____   Today's Thought _____
_____
_____

My thoughts and ideas _____
_____
_____
_____

Follow the 3 Rs:
1. Respect for self
2. Respect for others and
3. Responsibility for all your actions.

Name _____ **Date** _____

Respectful Thoughts

1. Number the days for this month.

2. Use these ideas as a guide for your daily journal writing.

MONDAY	TUESDAY	WEDNESDAY	THURSDAY	FRIDAY
"True politeness is perfect ease in freedom. It simply consists in treating others just as you love to be treated yourself." Earl of Chesterfield	"Whoever one is, and wherever one is, one is always in the wrong if one is rude." Maurice Baring	"Politeness is not always the sign of wisdom, but the want of it always leaves room for the suspicion of folly." Walter Savage Landor	"Rudeness is the weak man's imitation of strength." Eric Hoffer	"There can be no defense like elaborate courtesy." E.V. Lucas
"There can be no defense like elaborate courtesy." E.V. Lucas	"Human beings can alter their lives by altering their attitudes." William James	"I complained because I had no shoes until I met a man who had no feet." Arabic Proverb	"Do not remove a fly from your friend's forehead with a hatchet." Chinese Proverb	"He has the right to criticize who has the heart to help." Abraham Lincoln
"The best way to cheer yourself up is to try to cheer somebody else up." Mark Twain	"When fate hands up a lemon, let's try to make lemonade." Dale Carnegie	"Practice courtesy. You never know when it might become popular again." Bill Copeland	"Nothing is more becoming in a great man than courtesy and forbearance." Cicero	"Life is not so short but that there is always time enough for courtesy." Emerson
"My feeling is that there is nothing in life but refraining from hurting others, and comforting those that are sad." Oliver Schreiner	"You can get through life with bad manners, but it's easier with good manners." Lillian Gish	"To have respect for ourselves guides our morals; to have a deference for others governs our manners." Laurence Sterne	"Manners are the happy ways of doing things." Emerson	"Never underestimate the power of simple courtesy. Your courtesy may not be returned or remembered, but discourtesy will." Princess Jackson Smith

RS11b

Respect Ticket

To: _____

From: _____

Date: _____

THUMBS UP

This "THUMBS UP" is awarded because _____
_____

CONGRATULATIONS!
Please keep up your respectful behavior. It's appreciated.

- -

Respect Ticket

MEDAL OF HONOR

Awarded to _____

Dated _____

To get respect, you must earn respect.

You earned respect by _____
_____
_____
_____

Congratulations!

Respect Contract

Respect Projects

Directions: Choose any of the ideas below to create a project about respect. Show **WHAT** the trait means and **WHY** it is important to learn.

- mobile
- chart
- graph
- wind sock
- cube
- diorama
- movie
- puppet
- skit
- rap
- chant
- song
- rhyme
- cartoon
- poem
- play
- time line
- brochure
- news article
- want ad
- bumper sticker
- billboard
- headline
- relief map
- game
- backdrop
- transparency
- peek box
- banner
- newsletter
- photo album
- bulletin board
- interview

- tree map
- paper mache
- circle map
- spoke graph
- Venn diagram
- dance
- list
- charade
- calendar
- crossword puzzle
- letter
- advertisement
- display mural
- model
- debate
- painting
- pop-up book
- recipe
- riddle
- role play
- sculpture
- placemat
- motto
- survey
- media show
- maze
- mask
- hat
- paragraph
- scrapbook
- reader's theater
- pennant
- etching

- pamphlet
- constitution
- rubric
- stitchery
- ornament
- necklace
- oral report
- hanging
- commercial
- book jacket
- bookmark
- paperbag puppet
- jingle
- tongue twister
- tall tale
- myth or fairy tale
- menu
- campaign button
- telegram
- video
- mosaic
- book cube
- pantomime
- poster
- epitaph
- costume
- audio tape
- rebus
- journal
- announcement
- flag
- collage
- stamp

Respectful Openers!

"To get respect you must give respect"

RS14c

KEYS OF RESPECT

Respect like doors
will open with ease,
if you learn to
use these keys.

EXTINQUISH DISRESPECT!

BE RESPECTFUL · BE COURTEOUS · LISTEN · SHARE · ADMIRE · BE CONSIDERATE

APPROVE · BE THANKFUL · LISTEN · BE POLITE · BE UNDERSTANDING · SHARE · LISTEN · BE POLITE ·

SHARE · LISTEN · BE POLITE · BE UNDERSTANDING · SHARE · LISTEN · BE POLITE · BE THANKFUL · LISTEN · APPROVE · BE THANKFUL ·

NO DISRESPECT ZONE

Remember to ask yourself before you act: "Are my actions helpful or harmful?"

BE COMPLIMENTARY · LISTEN · BE CONSIDERATE · BE POLITE · BE COURTEOUS

RS20

SENDING COMPLIMENTS

1 STAND OR SIT STRAIGHT.

2 HOLD YOUR HEAD HIGH.

3 LOOK EYE TO EYE.

4 SAY YOUR COMPLIMENT LIKE YOU MEAN IT.

Permission to reprint for classroom use.
Character Builders, Jalmar Press
© 2001 by Michele Borba

RS22

'I LIKE' MESSAGES

(for sending respectful compliments)

I like + an earned quality.

1. "I like..."
Stand straight, hold your head high.
Look eye to eye.

2. + say an earned quality about the person you respect.

3. + tell why.

I LIKE HOW I CAN COUNT ON YOU!

RS24

ADMIRAL BOOK COVER
A GREETING FROM ALL OF US TO YOU!

Respect Motto: "To get respect you must give respect."

To: _____

From: _____

Date: _____

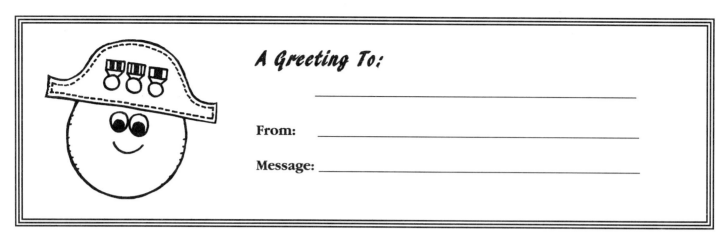

A Greeting To:

_____

From: _____

Message: _____

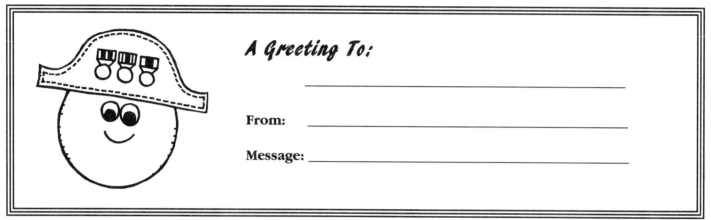

A Greeting To:

_____

From: _____

Message: _____

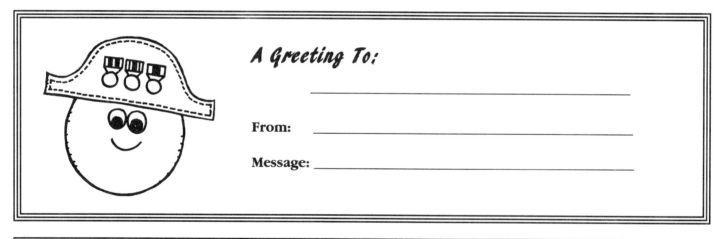

A Greeting To:

_____

From: _____

Message: _____

A Greeting To:

_____

From: _____

Message: _____

Name _____ Date _____

Pass It On Compliment

Rx for Respectful Compliment: **"I like + an earned quality."**

Write a respectful compliment to the owner of this paper on the first empty line. Now pass this page to the nearest classmate, who adds another compliment and passes it on.

I like _____

I like _____

I like _____

I like _____

I like _____

I like _____

I like _____

I like _____

Return this paper with a smile to the owner and make sure they say **"Thank you!"**

Respect Motto: To get respect you must give respect.

RECEIVING COMPLIMENTS

4 Steps to Receiving a Compliment

1. Look at the sender.
2. Hold your head high.
3. Use a clear voice.
4. Say "thank you" like you mean it.

"Thanks for noticing."   "Thanks!"
"Thank you."   "I value your opinion."
"I'm grateful."   "When you say that I feel good."
"I appreciate it when you…" "I appreciate that."
"That made me feel good."   "I really like it when you…"

RS28

Name —————

Date —————

A Month of Respect

Keep track of your own respectful statements. What did you do or say to put a smile on someone's face?

MONDAY	TUESDAY	WEDNESDAY	THURSDAY	FRIDAY

STUDENT GREETER

Ways to
Receive Compliments
"Thank you!"
"I appreciate that."
"That made me feel good."
"Thanks for noticing."
"I'm grateful."
"Thanks!"

TO GET RESPECT YOU MUST GIVE RESPECT

PARTNER SHARING

Taking turns to respectfully listen to each other's words.

Speaker
Use a calm 12" voice.
Look eye to eye.
Talk about the topic.
Hold your head high.

Listener
Sit still.
Look eye to eye.
No interrupting.
Think about what is being said.

RS 38

COMPANION READING

Listener

1. Listen respectfully.
2. Check for accuracy.
3. Encourage your partner.

Reader

1. Read!
2. Try your best.
3. Say, "Thank you."

RS 41

Permission to reprint for classroom use.
Character Builders, Jalmar Press
© 2001 by Michele Borba

Partner Recall

Letting the speaker know you understand the message.

Speaker
"I think…
"I heard you say…"
"Do you mean…?"
Use a calm 12" voice.
Hold your head high.
Look eye to eye.

Listener
"You said…"
"One think I heard you say…"
"I don't understand."
Don't interrupt.
Listen respectfully.
Look eye to eye.

RS 42

Interested Listener Comments

Comments

Date Used   Evaluation

"Really?"

"Thanks for sharing."

"That was interesting."

"I'd like to know more about..."

"Can you tell me more about..."

"I didn't know that."

"Why?"

"Is that so?"

"I see."

"Do you mean...?"

"I don't understand."

"Tell me more."

"Oh?"

"Then what?"

"Yes?"

"What happened next?"

"I wasn't sure what you meant when you said..."

RS 44a

Name _____ **Date** _____

I SAID　　YOU SAID

Topic _____
_____
_____
_____

I _____　　**You** _____

The main things I said:
_____
_____
_____
_____
_____
_____
_____
_____
_____
_____

The main things you said:
_____
_____
_____
_____
_____
_____
_____
_____
_____

Signed _____　　**Signed** _____

RS 44b

I SAID   YOU SAID

Name _____ Date _____

Respectful Listener Scorecard

Respectful Listening:

"Giving careful attention and consideration to another's words."

Team Member A:

Team Member B:

LISTENING SKILLS	A	B
Leaning Forward		
Eye Contact		
Nodding/Smiling		
Listening Respectfully		

Today's topic

My partner said

One thing I could do next time to improve my listening skills is

Partner A Name _____ Partner B Name _____ Date_____

RS 45a

Partner A Name _____ Partner B Name _____ Date_____

Respectful Listener Scorecord

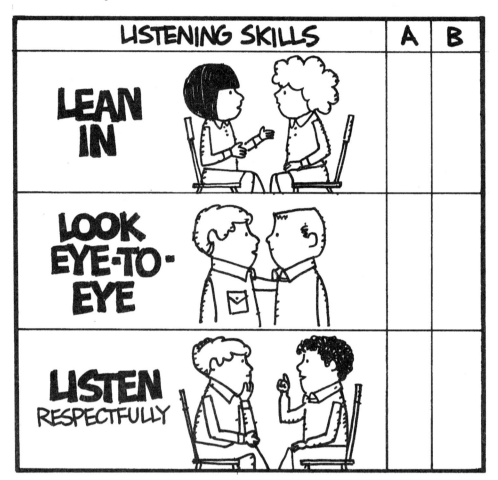

Today's topic was:

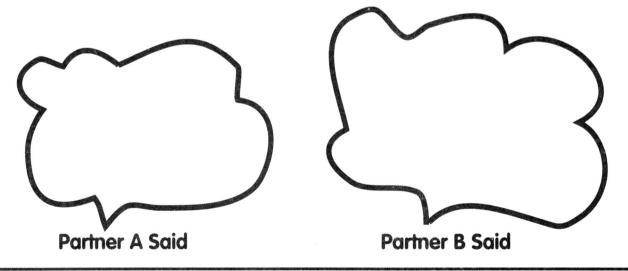

Partner A Said   **Partner B Said**

RESPECTFUL LISTENING AWARD

Presented to:_____

For demonstrating the skill of respectful listening.

*"Showing careful attention
to the words of a speaker."*

CONGRATULATIONS!

Signed _____

Date _____

LISTENING

BE RESPECTFUL • BE COURTEOUS • LISTEN • SHARE • ADMIRE • BE CONSIDERATE

LOOK

SIT QUIETLY

NOD

SMILE

RAISED EYEBROWS

HE LIKES BASEBALL

THINK ABOUT WHAT IS SAID

BE COMPLIMENTARY • LISTEN • BE CONSIDERATE • BE POLITE • BE COURTEOUS

BE RESPECTFUL • LISTEN • BE POLITE • BE UNDERSTANDING • SHARE • LISTEN • BE POLITE

APPROVE • BE THANKFUL • LISTEN • BE POLITE • BE UNDERSTANDING • SHARE • LISTEN • BE POLITE

APPROVE • BE THANKFUL • LISTEN • BE POLITE • BE UNDERSTANDING • SHARE • LISTEN • BE POLITE

Join Over a Half a Million Teachers and Parents for a Workshop by Dr. Borba
• Effective Teaching • Character Building • Parenting • Esteem Building • Moral Intelligence

Dr. Michele Borba's sessions are entertaining and enlightening, always provide real-life examples and proven solutions, and are guaranteed to change the way you deal with kids. Michele does keynote presentations, half-day, full-day, two-day and week-long training programs for your staff development and community training desires.

* You Are The Door Opener: A Keynote Address for Educators

This motivating and inspiring keynote explains why educators do have the power to impact their students' lives and help them reach their potential as learners. Using inspiring stories and real-life examples of teachers who are making a difference, educators are reminded they are door openers to a students' future because they offer five critical keys that maximize their students' success.

* Character Builders: How to Teach the Traits of Solid Character

Would you like your students to be more responsible and respectful? Then here's the program for you! Literally dozens of ways to enhance student character development are offered with a special emphasis on how to help students learn solid character behaviors and be more respectful and responsible. Monthly character themes that can be incorporated school-wide as well as in the classroom will also be shared and all ideas can be instantly integrated into subject content. Based on Dr. Borba's *Character Builders* program.

* Helping All Students Succeed: What Works!

The best teaching practices proven to help students learn more, behave better, be more engaged in their learning, and develop greater responsibility. While ALL students will benefit from the highly useful strategies shared, those with the most difficulties succeeding will especially benefit. Dozens of active learning techniques and quick processors to increase retention and nurture learning success are offered and all can enhance any subject at any grade level.

* Strengthening At-Risk Students' Achievement and Behavior

This seminar shares strategies for identifying high-risk students, and a wealth of proven techniques for strengthening their achievement, self-control, and motivation. Participants leave with dozens of practical strategies to help rebuild a cycle of success for our defeated youth that they can begin using tomorrow!

* Parents Do Make A Difference: A Special Parent Address

Parents learn practical ways to teach their children the eight critical traits of success: positive self-esteem, communicating, cultivating strengths, teamwork, problem-solving, goal-setting, perseverance, and caring. Practical ways to raise kids with solid character, strong minds and caring hearts are shared. Based on Dr. Borba's book *Parents do Make A Difference*.

* Esteem Building: Increasing Achievement, Behavior and Learning Climates

Practical strategies for identifying and helping low esteem students and a model for esteem-building based on the five building blocks identified in Dr. Borba's best-selling book, *Esteem Builders*. Dozens of classroom-proven techniques and activities to strengthen their classroom environment to enhance students' self esteem and in the process improve their students' behavior and achievement are offered.

* Building Moral Intelligence: Our Last Best Hope

Moral intelligence is the growing capacity to decipher right from wrong, choose what's right then behave morally and teaching it may be our best hope for preventing peer cruelty, violence, and anti-social behaviors. This session explores the latest research that confirms how teaching moral intelligence can enhance our students' prosocial behaviors and replace negative ones and provides practical strategies that can easily be implemented in any program that teach students the essential moral behaviors of empathy, conscience, self-control, respect, kindness, tolerance, and fairness. Based on Dr. Borba's latest book, *Building Moral Intelligence*.

Contact Dr. Borba at Office/fax (760)323-5387 • E-mail BorbaM@aol.com
A complete list of sessions is available on Dr. Borba's website: www.Moralintelligence.com

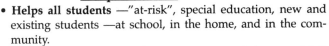

ORDER FORM

Customer Service Hotline
(800)662-9662

Ordered by:
Name _____
School/Company_____
Address_____
City_____State___Zip_____

Ship to:
Name _____
School/Company_____
Address_____
City_____State___Zip_____

Check payment method used:
__ Check enclosed.　　___VISA　　__MasterCard　　___Discover　　__AMEX
　　　　　　　　　　Card Number _____ Exp. Date _____
　　　　　　　　　　Signature (as it appears on card) _____

Purchase order #_____
Please attach your purchase order to completed order form.

For fastest service call toll free (800)662-9662, 24 hours a day, 7 days a week!

MAIL OR FAX YOUR ORDER TO:
JALMAR PRESS
P. O. BOX 1185
TORRANCE, CA 90505
(310)816-3092

Character Builders	Order #	Price	Qty	Total
Responsibility and Trustworthiness	JP9654	$19.95	___	$____
Respect for Self and Others	JP9655	$19.95	___	$____
Fairness and Cooperation*	JP9656	$19.95	___	$____
Caring*	JP9658	$19.95	___	$____
Positive Attitudes and Peacemaking	JP9659	$19.95	___	$____

*Not available yet.

Each volume 200 pages, 8-1/2" x 11", filled with illustrations, posters and activities.

Esteem Builders' Complete Program	Order#	Price	Qty	Total
Esteem Builders, paperback	JP9053	$39.95	___	$____
Esteem Builders, spiral	JP9088	$49.95	___	$____
Staff Esteem Builders	JP9604	$44.95	___	$____
Home Esteem Builders	JP9065	$34.95	___	$____
Resources for EBCP	JP9625	$34.95	___	$____
Overview of EBCP	JP9600	$44.95	___	$____
Trainer's Manual	JP9078	$129.95	___	$____
Esteem Builders Posters	JP9605	$18.95	___	$____
Five Building Blocks, Audios	JP9622	$89.95	___	$____
EBCP Complete Program Kit	JP9086	$448.60	___	$____

Subtotal $_____
California residents add sales tax _____
Add 10% for shipping (minimum $5.00)_____
TOTAL$ _____

Order on the internet: www.jalmarpress.com or e-mail to: jalmarpress@att.net